# God's Plan for Living

A Simple Roadmap to Your IDEAL Kingdom Life

Matt Tommey

**God's Plan for Living:** A Simple Roadmap to Your IDEAL Kingdom Life
Matt Tommey Copyright © 2023 Matt Tommey. All rights reserved.

www.GodsPlanForLiving.com

Unless otherwise quoted, all Scripture quotations are from the Holy Bible, New King James Version, (NKJV). Copyright © 1982. Thomas Nelson, Inc.

Scripture quotations marked (NIV) are from the Holy Bible, New International Version. Copyright © 1973, 1978, 1984, International Bible Society.

Scripture quotations marked (ESV) are from The Holy Bible, English Standard Version®, copyright © 2001 by Crossway, a publishing ministry of Good News Publishers. Used by permission. All rights reserved.

Scripture quotations marked (NLT) are from the Holy Bible, New Living Translation. Copyright ©1996 by Tyndale House Publishers, Inc., Wheaton, IL 60189.

Scripture quotations marked (KJV) are from the King James Version of the Bible.

ISBN-13: 979-8378290628

# Table of Contents

# Introduction

Somehow, this whole thing just got complicated. The simple message of Jesus, sent from the Father to redeem the world and restore humanity to His loving embrace, has morphed into an endless list of dos and don'ts, preferences and traditions that have put the promises of God on the shelf and much of the church into program-oriented or personality-driven irrelevance. And what's worse, most Christians—committed as they may be—have no clue how to step into the abundant life that Jesus promised in John 10:10. Leaders often speak in platitudes and phrases that sound spiritual. People try to remain faithful. And still, no one actually knows how to implement simple Kingdom truths into their life to experience lasting transformation.

That individual and corporate frustration has resulted in a declining church with little actual power whose members are simply trying to do their best to live a "good Christian life"— never having been taught how to access the power and strategies that make that available. Regular everyday Christians that aren't involved in professional, vocational ministry are left feeling like second-class citizens, searching for their place in the Kingdom.

Living in that frustration was my experience for many, many years. But thankfully, I started learning how the Kingdom of God works through many great Bible teachers, study, personal experiences and spending extended time with the Lord. Once I discovered the reality of the Kingdom for myself and all its power, principles and benefits—my life completely changed. I don't mean it changed a little bit or that I got Holy Spirit goosebumps during a church service. I mean everything tangibly changed. It started with the healing of my heart and moved quickly into my overall mindset about life, myself, God and how I related to others. Once my personal life started changing, I began to see major changes in my business, my financial life and ultimately my opportunities to make a difference in the world.

Over a period of years, my whole life completely changed from one plagued by frustration, striving and discontent, to one filled with joy and fulfillment. I was finally able to embrace my unique design and the passionate pursuit of my God-given assignment. As I began sharing what I was learning with others, their lives started changing as well, regardless of who they were, where they were in the world, or what their past looked like. The same can be true for you as well. You can absolutely experience the fullness of God's original intent for your life and this book is going to show you how.

I promise you friend, by the time you finish this book, you will know how to step into God's very best for your life without any religious hype, secret formulas, or performance traps. I'm going to share a pathway right out of God's Word that, when followed with faith and expectation in your heart, will transform your life. The principles of God's IDEAL happen simultaneously in our journey with Jesus—both the operation and the maturing as we are led by the Holy Spirit. You don't have to master one area to move into another or have permission to operate in another before mastering one. It's like a corkscrew of growth toward God rather than a series of gates you must pass through to have permission to move forward.

And if you're one of those people who loves to get down on yourself because you're not doing everything perfectly, then let me put your heart at rest. While I do believe the principles I'm going to teach you are in line with God's IDEAL for your life in the Kingdom, you must embrace the fact we're all in process. You're in a process. I'm in the process. Nobody on the earth is walking in the fullness of this right now. Only Jesus did that. But like Paul said in Philippians 3:12-14 NLT, *"I don't mean to say that I have already achieved these things or that I have already reached perfection. But I press on to possess that perfection for which Christ Jesus first possessed me. No, dear brothers and sisters, I have not achieved it, but I focus on this one thing: Forgetting the past and looking forward to what lies ahead, I press on to reach the end of the race and receive the heavenly prize for which God, through Christ Jesus, is calling us."*

If you're ready for the journey, then let's press on.

# Chapter 1

*The Great Disconnect*

When I became a Christian many years ago as a young teen, there was no simple how-to manual for how this thing called "being a Christian" worked. I got saved, got a new leather study Bible with my name embossed in gold leaf and I was good to go. As most people do, I simply jumped in line with what I saw around me. I went to church, followed the rules, tried my best not to live in overt sin and hoped one day God's plan for my life would be realized. But there was always a feeling of discontent in my heart because the things I saw promised and promoted in God's Word were rarely the things I saw showing up in my life or the lives of those around me.

Consequently, I subconsciously accepted the abundant life that Jesus promised—full of signs, wonders, fulfillment, provision, opportunity, resources, relationships, calling, healing, miracles and impact—wasn't available to everyone—just to a select few. Who that select few were, nobody seemed to know. But one thing was for sure: I wasn't included. The decision on who was blessed and who wasn't seemed to be relegated to spiritual platitudes: the realm of God's sovereignty and when or how He chose to bless someone. If you've experienced this mindset, you know how disempowering and disconnecting it can be. Your left wondering why God blesses some and not others. Does God love them more? Why doesn't He answer my prayers?

This is the Great Disconnect. It's why most Christians are walking around, as the old saying goes "broke, busted and disgusted," trying their best to live a life that's pleasing to God but having no real clarity on how it happens. And to complicate matters even further, it's the plan of the enemy to keep believers separated from all that is ours in the Kingdom as restored sons and daughters. Unless we reconnect to the Father through His son Jesus and fully understand how the Kingdom works, we'll continue to experience life far below what the Father intended.

As a part of preparing to write this book, I surveyed hundreds of Christians regarding their ability to know and pursue God's plan for their life. They were from a variety of Christian streams with a variety of religious and life experiences. Men and women, young, middle-aged and elderly from all around the world. The results I received were astounding but unfortunately, not surprising.

The vast majority of people reported struggling greatly with the concept of knowing God's plan for their life. Based on their religious upbringing and life experience, many wondered if it was even possible to know God's plan. Consequently, their lives did not reflect the abundant life Jesus promised. Instead, they reported feeling confused, frustrated and often overwhelmed, causing them to feel discouraged, alone and like a disappointment to themselves, others and God. Most said they had difficulty hearing God's voice. And many reported feeling a failure, that their best years were either behind them or wasted.

Those who did believe God had a plan for their life experienced major difficulty when it came to pursuing that plan. Either they didn't know how or didn't have the confidence to do so on a daily basis. They felt anxious and inadequately prepared for what God was calling them to.

In light of this myriad of emotions, they used a variety of strategies to keep going in their walk with the Lord. Some were going to the Lord and Holy Spirit for direction, but the majority felt hopeless and reported using dead-end strategies like self-medicating, striving, following the crowd and yielding to feelings of depression.

Before we move on, I want you to let this reality sink in. Hundreds and hundreds of people who love Jesus and are doing everything they know to do feel utterly defeated and unable to connect with God's best for their life—despite their committed hearts and best efforts. Most are actively pursuing their faith and do things like attend church every week. They volunteer, teach Sunday school and even sing on the worship team. Yet they're completely disillusioned, faithful but frustrated. Multiply that reality across the Body of Christ worldwide along with its paralyzing impact and I believe it's potentially the greatest issue facing the church today. No wonder we see people leaving organized religion in droves. Why would they stay? The authentic influence of the church is waning as its people are merely going through the motions.

And if I had to guess, there's a good chance you are in that same category, just like I was for many years. Loving Jesus, hoping for more, but having no idea how to walk in the victorious life God promised us in His Word. Living a life of mediocrity, with hope low and expectations lower. Don't let the enemy throw shame on you—

but I'm here to tell you, this "normal Christian life" you're living is not God's normal for you.

Imagine the Father's heartbreak, watching His children living lives of frustration, striving and performing, all the while knowing that He, through Jesus, has already restored them to His original intent. Imagine Jesus seeing those He died to restore choosing to walk in their own strength, struggling and striving every day when they have already been given all things. Imagine the Holy Spirit waiting to guide us on an ultimate divine adventure and all the while, we don't even know a Spirit-led adventure is an option. This great disconnect is keeping the church powerless, ineffective, frustrated and lifeless.

The enemy doesn't have to tempt you with overt sin to defeat you. He simply has to convince you that you're not good enough, smart enough, qualified enough, healed enough, or spiritual enough to step into God's glorious plan for your life. If he can do that, he's made a major step toward defeating you. How? Because everything you do will be based on proving your worth to yourself, God and others or hiding because of your deep feelings of inadequacy. Either way, you're not living in the confident assurance that you're God's beloved child.

## The Gospel of Salvation vs the Gospel of the Kingdom

So how did this disconnect emerge? Well, it starts with the fact that most Christians are taught a salvation-centric view of the Christian life rather than the holistic view of the Kingdom found in God's Word. Consequently, it places the salvation experience at the center of the Christian's life, rather than seeing salvation as the doorway to the Kingdom and restoration's promise.

*The enemy doesn't have to tempt you with overt sin to defeat you.*

Don't get me wrong. I'm not saying there is any other way to the Father than through His son Jesus and Him crucified. Jesus said in John 14:6 NIV, *"I am the way and the truth and the life. No one comes to the Father **except** through me."* That is not up for debate. It's a settled fact. But, to center your life around that salvation experience only, without recognizing the fact that the whole point of salvation is not only to redeem you (thank you Lord!) but also to reconcile you to relationship with the Father and restore you to the fullness of God's original intent for your life as His son or daughter in the Kingdom, is truly missing two-thirds of the benefits of your salvation experience.

To further clarify, there's a comparison chart on the next page that may make things a bit clearer:

| Gospel of Salvation | Gospel of the Kingdom |
|---|---|
| Get saved primarily to escape eternal damnation and separation from God. | Get saved as an invitation to be redeemed from sin, reconciled to the Father and restored as His child. |
| Believe your primary focus in life should be making sure everyone is converted and coming to church through overt evangelism and church-centered activities. | Believe your primary focus in life should be "*doing the things you see the Father doing*" in line with God's unique design for your life as led by the Holy Spirit. |
| Focus most of your attention on your eternal hope of heaven after death and escaping the trappings of "this old world". | Focus most of your attention on releasing the Kingdom now through your unique design while led and empowered by the Holy Spirit. |
| Hold on patiently until Jesus comes. | Enjoy abundant Kingdom life, knowing the best is yet to come as you co-labor with God in every area of life. |

Jesus didn't just come to open the door to heaven that was locked as a result of your sin. He came to open the door to all the fullness of His Father's Kingdom and to bring you into the abundant life He has promised. An abundant life for now and in the life to come. He came to bring you into a new reality—the reality of the Kingdom.

As you can see, the difference is clear! Life as a Christian without an understanding of how the Kingdom works leads to treating every person you meet as a project. A transactional relationship where you try to score an immediate evangelistic win, rather than an opportunity to show the Love of God, sow into their life and be a part of that person's journey toward coming to know Christ as the Holy Spirit draws them. It leads to second-guessing your unique calling and design if you don't fit the traditional church mold of what ultimate success as a Christian looks like including being a missionary or local church leader.

Believe me, I know that reality all too well and the patterns of living it creates. Every day, another climb on the religious treadmill. And it's a fundamental misunderstanding of how the Kingdom of God works. It might lead to higher church attendance and volunteerism among the faithful, but rarely does it result in long-term transformation.

## 3 Common Models of Living

When Christians try to live the Christian life outside of understanding the Kingdom, there are essentially three models of living they adopt to make life manageable. I don't mean to suggest that people who live like this are intentionally living in sin. These common models of living develop mostly out of desperation to live a Spirit-led life. Unfortunately, living life from our best understanding based on our past circumstances, the circumstances of others and how positive or negatively those are interpreted—does not bring us the results we want. Viewing things through an inner framework that is not based in God's Word creates frustration and confusion, rather than enabling us to live in victory. This was my story. Maybe you can relate.

## Wait, Hope & Beg

The "wait, hope and beg" model of living seems really spiritual on the surface. In fact, I'd say it's what most Christians default to because it's what we learned growing up. It is often the root of phrases like, "I'm just waiting on the Lord."

A common belief pattern that supports this model and has unfortunately become a normal way of life for most believers is: God is in control of everything so I don't have to do anything. I know I can relate to this one! After all, we are His servant and if God want's something to happen in our life, He'll bring it about at the right time. Our part is to wait patiently on God and hope what He brings to us in His perfect timing will be good. When the waiting gets to be too much, it's common to throw in some fervent begging, reminding God how badly we need a breakthrough. Ultimately, we go back to waiting.

However, even for the most committed, this quickly gets frustrating and leads to a "waiting ON God" mindset instead of getting to know God's heart and walking out life WITH God. Remember, the Bible says, "*hope deferred makes the heart sick.*" It's a common way of living but definitely not God's ideal.

## Work, Sweat & Strive

That leads me to a second common model of living for believers who don't yet understand how the Kingdom of God works. It is the "work, sweat and strive" model. When the waiting, hoping and begging fails, we then try to make things happen in our own strength. Of course, that's a natural response. It comes right out of the curse Adam and Eve experienced when sin caused them to be banished from the Garden of Eden.

A common belief pattern in the "work, sweat and strive" model of living is: God helps those who help themselves. And, since God seems to be a little slow, it only makes sense in the natural to take matters into our own hands and get some forward momentum going. A core belief develops—succeeding in life is hard work and to succeed, you must hustle, grind and make it happen—whatever it takes!

Yep, I've been there! Thinking some action was better than no action, I modeled my life after my best ideas or what others were doing that seemed successful. Striving in my own strength, I became performance and productivity oriented and eventually exhausted. Not what I would call the abundant life.

## Get, Do & Live

A third model of living, even more rooted in striving, is a general belief that one must attain certain status, success, notoriety, opportunities, resources, or relationships in order to do the thing God has called them to do. And once we do, we'll finally become the person God designed us to be and live the life God called us to live.

Common beliefs and patterns in this model of living include the belief we must build a big platform so people know who we are or we won't accomplish God's will for our life. Or conversely, we need to make enough money or retire <u>before</u> we can pursue what God has put on our hearts. Often the act of doing and being productive for God defines our self and perceived worth in the eyes of others and God. Busyness is often equated to godliness. If one is not being productive (as exemplified by being constantly busy) and "working for the Lord" then they are not honoring God.

Again, yes, I've been there! Paralyzed because what I thought I needed wasn't showing up. It's only out of a healthy cooperative relationship with the Father lasting fruit can be produced in our lives—fruit that not only blesses us but is also a conduit of transformation for others.

## The Enemy at Work

From the beginning of time, the enemy has been at work, devising plans to disconnect us from the Father. His primary strategies; lying and sowing doubt. With these two tools he seduced Adam and Eve into believing the lie: their Father didn't have their best interests at heart. He sowed a seed of doubt into their hearts. A seed that grew into the fruit of unbelief, ultimately resulting in sin. Instead of choosing to believe in the goodness of God, they believed the enemy's seduction—they had been tricked by God and He was holding out on them. The enemy uses this same strategy on us today.

When we choose to believe the lies of the enemy over the promises of God and struggle and strive on our own, we close the door to God and open the door for the enemy to come in and wreak havoc. Frustration grows when we allow our problems, fears and worries to appear bigger than God's promises.

*Frustration grows
when we allow our
problems, fears and worries
to appear bigger than
God's promises.*

God is a God of restoration. And from the fall of humanity in Genesis through the finished work of Jesus on the cross, God's heart has always been to bring His children back to Him. To restore what the enemy stole through their sin. And how did the Father accomplish that restorative work? Through the cross of Jesus. The purpose of Jesus' birth, life, death, burial and resurrection was always restoration. John 3:16-18 NIV, says it best, *"For God so loved the world that He gave His one and only Son, that whoever believes in Him shall not perish but have eternal life. [17] For God did not send His Son into the world to condemn the world, but to save the world through Him. [18] Whoever believes in Him is not condemned, but whoever does not believe stands condemned already because they have not believed in the name of God's one and only Son."*

But in order to be restored, humanity first had to be redeemed from death, hell and the grave and reconciled back into relationship with the Father. The word "saved" in John 3:17 is the Greek word sozo which means saved, rescued, healed and preserved. It's a full work of restoration. To preach the gospel without restoration is like telling the story of the prodigal son without giving him back his inheritance. Glad you made it back alive. Now get back to work and don't forget, your rent is due on Friday.

When you read the Gospels through the eyes of religion, it's easy to think God calls people to become obedient robots. Deny yourself. Become less so He can become greater. Not my will but His be done. It can feel like you have nothing to offer. Like you'll never measure up. Like you just need to get in line, get saved, be glad you are and don't expect anything else until Heaven.

But when we read the Gospels through the perspective of the Kingdom, everything changes. The Father didn't send Jesus to force humanity into obedience simply to avoid eternal damnation— although that is a glorious benefit of our salvation through Christ. He doesn't require us to only experience suffering here while we wait on heaven's benefits and blessings. Jesus was sent to awaken our hearts to the reality of the Father's Love. Invite us into a reconciled relationship with the Father. Redeem us from our sin and all its deadly consequences. Restore us as children of God with all its blessings and benefits. By ourselves, we could never achieve any of this. But through Christ, all these things are given to us as a free gift. Even though Jesus reminded us we will have trouble in this life, we can overcome. Not by our own strength but empowered by His grace. The same power that raised Jesus from the grave lives inside us. That's good news!

Jesus' prayer in Luke 22:42, *"not my will but yours be done,"* was a humble declaration of His commitment to walking through unimaginable difficulty in the context of a loving, trusting relationship with the Father. Jesus' call in Matthew 16:24, to deny ourselves, take up our cross and follow Him is an invitation to shed the self-reliance, self-interest and performance identity that came as a result of sin's curse. To embrace life in relationship with Him. Jesus reminds us in Mathew 16:25, that, *"...whoever wants to save their life would end up losing it but whoever gives up their life for Him would find it." (NIV)* True life is not found in trying to rescue yourself by any means necessary but in trusting completely in Him to be saved, delivered and healed. John the Baptist's declaration in John 3:30, that he must decrease and Jesus must increase, was a reminder that this is God's story, not ours. We have a part to play, but we're not the star of the show. The story includes us but it's not about us.

To embrace Jesus and the message of the Gospel demands we release the self-reliance and self-protection we've relied upon in the past and pursue a new way of living. A way based on walking with Him in a relationship as we listen, trust, defer to and act in faith.

When we understand the Gospel in terms of God's desire for a relationship with humanity, everything changes. Jesus' life, death and resurrection is seen as an invitation to more than one could ask or imagine, rather than just an escape hatch to avoid hell.

Unfortunately, many churches preach a partial gospel—not because they have bad intentions but simply because it's what they know. It's a message focused solely on getting saved so you don't go to hell, rather than walking in the fullness of everything Jesus died to restore to us. A way to prove your love for God through works—rather than the joy filled freedom of co-laboring with Him through our unique design. Oh, my friend, there's so much more!

## *Salvation opens the door to the fullness of the Kingdom.*

The story of the Prodigal Son personifies the beauty of the new covenant gospel and reveals how happy it makes the Father when we return to Him out of desire rather than obligation. God the Father runs toward those who are lost and generously restores all that our sinful selfish desires wasted, even though we don't deserve it. God desires to mend relationships and reestablish family bonds, even when we run away from Him. It proves God's commitment to fully re-establish us to the place He originally designed us for—with all provision, authority and opportunity needed to thrive. That's the gospel and that's why it's truly good news.

## The Kingdom Changes Everything

God's original intent is that we walk in the fullness of His Kingdom as His children; fully restored, receiving everything we need for life and godliness in abundance by faith. And the implications are bigger than you think. It's an invitation into His grand story of restoration.

As I was reflecting on this great invitation, I was reminded of something that happened to me years ago on a ministry trip. I was invited down to a west Texas town to minister for the weekend and in between sessions, we had some down time. My host graciously invited me to visit their ranch for the afternoon and I was excited to see it. As we left town and got out into the country, it seemed like we were in the middle of nowhere. Nothing around, just fences and tumbleweeds. After making conversation, I finally asked if we were getting close? They laughed and reassured me we had arrived. They'd just wanted me to have a chance to take in the view.

A few more minutes of driving brought us through a gate and then up to the house.

It was a gorgeous Texas ranch overlooking incredible mountain plateaus and canyons. I was gob smacked. When I asked how far their property went, they pointed to the horizon and said their land extended as far as I could see. It was more than I could have ever imagined. In fact, I didn't even have a grid for something like it—much less had the opportunity to experience something like this without an invitation from the owner.

The same opportunity awaits us in the Kingdom of God. It's so much bigger and better than we could ever imagine. And, we've been invited into it by our Father. But not as a visitor or an observer—as God's child with full rights and privileges to all it encompasses. You and I are part of the family.

I know all this may seem too good to be true, but I promise, it's not! This is God's IDEAL, the Kingdom life He designed for us before the very foundation of the world. And the life Jesus died and rose to restore us to. In the next chapter, we'll uncover more about God's IDEAL and how you can step into its reality.

# Chapter 2

*God's IDEAL*

When God created the world and humanity, He didn't just throw a bunch of mud, minerals and gases up in the ether and hope for the best. He had a plan, a dream and an ideal. I believe there was a picture in His mind of what this place, these people and their experience could be like when empowered by a life-giving relationship with Him. Don't forget,

## *The first way God revealed Himself to humanity was as an artist.*

He is a creator, and like all creators, He started with the end in mind. And it wasn't just hope alone, but hope mixed with faith. Since He knows the end from the beginning and is Himself, the Alpha and Omega, God had full faith that the plans He held in His heart would be realized. When He spoke His hope into existence, the universe was formed. When God breathed life into Adam, the potential God envisioned was deposited into his being, ready to be activated as he walked with the Father. The ideal that had once existed only in the heart of God now became a reality.

When the Lord first spoke to me about this concept of His IDEAL, the first thing that came to mind was the phrase "the ideal vs the real". In other words, I had a picture of what the ideal could be but I wasn't about to get my hopes up, some things are just too good to be true. That ideal was unrealistic and impossible for me. But as I shifted my mindset into agreement with God—in Christ, all things are possible to those who believe—I started to understand what I'm about to teach you.

God's ideal is not an unachievable goal only a few can reach. It's God's best for everyone. And we don't have to try and figure it out on our own. We've been given a clear picture in God's Word of what an ideal life in Christ looks like along with the promise of the Holy Spirit's leadership to help us walk it out. Inside the pages of this book, I'm going to reveal that ideal in a way that will cause your faith to grow toward every Kingdom thing God has planned for you. No matter where you come from or how old or young you are, there's no reason every Christian can't walk in God's ideal right now. That doesn't mean you'll never have another struggle or another area of your life to mature in, but it does mean that you'll experience His empowering grace as you learn to walk in God's ideal.

## What is God's IDEAL?

Through my own personal study, life experience and having mentored thousands of believers over the years, I've come to believe there are five principles that embody the ideal God has for each one of His children. When combined, these five principles create a simple framework for living and thriving in God's Kingdom that can be used by anyone, at any time, to start experiencing accelerated transformation in their life.

## *Lasting transformation in the Kingdom happens from the inside out.*

The Apostle John knew this when he said in 3 John 2 KJV, *"Beloved, I wish above all things that thou mayest prosper and be in health, even as thy soul prospereth."* He understood that prospering externally was the fruit of prospering internally.

And that's what God's IDEAL is all about. Instead of just waiting for a breakthrough to happen, we can learn to cultivate an atmosphere of breakthrough and walk in continual breakthrough as our normal operating procedure. And when we do, we become a carrier of all the Kingdom's blessings and benefits.

As we unpack each part of God's IDEAL, you'll begin to understand how each principle works together, building on each other to create a beautiful, mature and unique expression of the Kingdom of God in and through your life. These principles are like the 5 smooth stones of David. Five principles for Kingdom living that will enable you to slay the giants of fear, frustration, inadequacy and doubt while empowering you to live in all the fullness God designed for you.

To help you understand this framework for living, I've created a simple acronym for the word IDEAL:

- **Identity:** Believe who God says you are
- **Design:** Know and celebrate your unique God-given design
- **Expansion:** Walk fearlessly into ALL God has called you to
- **Alignment:** How God positions you & how you respond
- **Love:** Be anchored in & motivated by God's great Love

Before we jump into how these principles work individually, I want to tell you why I've assembled this framework in this order.

As I mentioned in the previous chapter, most people are used to either waiting on God and doing nothing or striving in their own strength without inviting God into their day-to-day living. You also saw from the survey results I shared earlier that most people live in frustration, disappointment and overwhelm despite being committed Christians. Not because they don't love Jesus or aren't trying to pursue Him daily, but because they don't understand how the Kingdom of God really works or how to apply Kingdom principles in their life. Thankfully, we're about to change that for you.

## Identity is Your Foundation

In God's IDEAL, everything starts with identity. It's the foundation for everything in Kingdom living. Until we know who we are in Christ—we'll allow everyone and everything around us to define us. Living life on autopilot and reaction mode instead of intentionally pursuing what's promised to you in the Kingdom. Even though

God's Plan for Living | Matt Tommey

that's how most people live their life, it's a recipe for a lifetime of frustration.

Although precise definitions vary, most dictionaries refer to identity as our sense of self. Who we believe ourselves to be based on the experiences, characteristics, beliefs, roles and qualities that make up our lives. But as a believer in Christ, we have been transformed into a whole new creation. Our identity no longer comes from external things, our feelings, or the opinions of others. It comes from who God says we are. Whereas before, our identity was on a shifting foundation, in Christ it's now secure and unchanging.

Embracing our new identity means embracing who God says we are along with what He says is possible for us in the Kingdom. Our disappointments, mistakes and regrets no longer have the right to determine our future. The slate has been wiped clean.

## Divine Design

Secondly, as God's children, we reflect Him on the earth with our unique perspective—how we see the world, others and all that's possible in this life. God has filled each of us with gifts and graces to further expand our capacity for both influence and fulfillment. His purpose for each of us is to bear His image to others and be an ambassador of Kingdom transformation in the world. Once you embrace who God says you are—your new identity in Christ—the uniqueness with which He's designed you will reflect God's unique nature to all who encounter you. Instead of trying to be like everyone else, you focus on becoming the real you. That's liberating.

God's IDEAL | 25

## Expanding Your Horizon

Expansion is the next piece in the framework because it's the natural fruit of faithfulness to our identity and design. This is where our Kingdom assignment emerges. Everything we are called to do in the Kingdom should be birthed from intimacy with God, not religious obligation, or personal zeal. Why? Because nothing of eternal value can be accomplished unless you know who you are in Him (identity), how He's uniquely created you (design) and that you are empowered by His Spirit. Otherwise, we end up performing and striving on our own. As we are faithful to walk with Him, God brings expansion, multiplication and promotion in the context of our assignment.

## Perfect Alignment

Next in the IDEAL framework is alignment and here's how it works. As we cultivate our identity in Christ, embrace our unique design and begin to walk with God in the calling He has entrusted to us—God supernaturally aligns us with the ideas, opportunities, resources and relationships we need. This isn't something we have to beg or compete for. It's the natural outflow of our relationship with Him. God would never give us a vision without empowering us with everything we need to accomplish it. Of course not! He's the God of more than enough. More than we can think or imagine! He gives us eyes to see, ears to hear and the ability to recognize times and seasons. He brings the right people to the right place at the right time. Instead of striving to make things happen on our own, or living with a scarcity-based poverty mentality—God provides everything we need in abundance.

God also aligns us through His process of refinement. Throughout our journey, the Father will allow circumstances to challenge our old mindsets and way of living. This is the Father's way of showing us what we need to let go of in order to step fully into His very best. Your choice to cooperate or resist these moments of refining will have a major impact on how fast you'll grow in the Kingdom.

## Love is the Glue

The last part of the IDEAL framework is love because it's the glue that holds everything together. Everything in the Kingdom flows from love. Love of God, love for others, a healthy love for ourselves and a love for the things God has called us to accomplish for His Glory. Without the Love of God as the primary motivating factor in our life, motives can be skewed. Next thing you know we're off in left field, pursuing an agenda that has little to do with lasting Kingdom impact.

Without the Love of God as our anchor, we'll view opportunities, resources and people through our natural understanding, rather than through the eyes of divine purpose. But when we learn to operate from a place of identity and design, God expands our opportunities and aligns us with everything we need to accomplish His plans and purposes for our life as we walk in His Love. All while leading us into maturity in Him.

I wish I could say I recognized this IDEAL framework early on in my journey with the Lord, but that's not the case. I didn't know God was trying to establish these things in my life so I could thrive in His Kingdom. I was a striver. I operated out of self-protection. I doubted my own potential and didn't understand who God said I was as a man. Unfortunately, it took me many years of struggle and frustration to start recognizing how these Kingdom principles really worked. Once I did, everything clicked. I started seeing them all over the place. In my own life and in the lives of my friends. In those I mentored and throughout the stories of men and women in God's Word.

## A Picture of God's IDEAL

One of the best examples of God's IDEAL at work is in the life of David. Twice in the Bible, David is referred to as a "man after God's own heart". That doesn't mean he was perfect by any means. But I do believe that despite the difficulties and challenges he faced, the trajectory of David's heart and life was moving toward God. Like you and me, he was a person on a journey with a Father who loved him deeply.

I can so relate to David because the difficulties publicly displayed in David's life were rooted in identity issues. Think about it. Why would David seek out Bathsheba – another man's wife – when he had everything he wanted as King? Was it because he felt empty in some area and needed someone to affirm his identity? Maybe at the root, David felt unloved despite being called a man after God's own heart and being known as a lover of God.

But as much as David struggled with that, it was his practice to remind himself who he was, who God was and all He had promised. I love Psalm 43:5 NLT where David encourages himself, *"Why am I discouraged? Why is my heart so sad? I will put my hope in God! I will praise Him again— my Savior and my God!"* He knew that unless he continuously reoriented his mind to God's truth, he would struggle alone in his own strength. Walking in a healthy identity for David wasn't a one-time decision, but an intentional daily choice.

Throughout the Biblical narrative, we also see the beautiful uniqueness of David's design as a worshipper and creative person, as well as a natural leader. And judging from the stories we know: he was intuitive, empathetic, passionate and brave. Talk about a unique human being! Of course, the enemy tried to wound him in those areas to keep him from walking in his unique design. Satan didn't want David to reflect God's nature on the earth and he doesn't want us too either.

But just because David had an assignment and anointing, doesn't mean there wasn't some significant growth that needed to happen. As David abided with God in the secret place of worship and walked through the refining situations of life, he matured in the Lord. His connection with God deepened and His identity was further established as one loved by God.

God brought David into alignment with the right people, opportunities and resources to both refine and position him for greater effectiveness. He had to fight some bears and lions along the way. He had to face a giant, overcome the lust of the flesh and he even served a King who ended up wanting to destroy him. Not an easy road. But through it all, David persevered. And he was blessed with all he needed to accomplish that which God had placed on his heart.

Though he made mistakes, acted immaturely and stumbled along the way, David continued to worship and walk with God. His love for God remained foundational. The presence of God enabled David to live a brave and courageous life of impact and influence for the Glory of God we are still talking about today. That's God's IDEAL at work.

The life of David demonstrates God's commitment to walk with us through the process of ongoing maturity rather than expecting complete perfection. It proves His heart is for relationship rather than performance. Knowing those things about our heavenly Father gives me a lot of hope and creates the space where grace-filled living emerges. Life without the pressure to perform. Life without the heavy yoke of religious obligation. Life committed to walking with Him each day rather than performing for Him. I hope David's story inspires hope in your heart as well.

Each of these ideal concepts – identity, design, expansion, alignment, love – have always existed in the Word of God. But I hope that by bringing them together in one simple framework for living, they will help change your perspective and cause you to look at life in the Kingdom of God in a completely different way. One that's not limited by your denominational experience, wounded past, or limiting beliefs about yourself. One that's possible and accessible to you as one deeply loved by God. I pray as you start pursuing the Kingdom of God, you begin to experience the kind of Spirit-birthed convergence so many other believers and I are experiencing. A dynamic so rich and so transforming you'll wonder why nobody shared this with you before.

## An Overflow Effect

The implications of God's IDEAL go far beyond the life of the individual believer. In this hour, God is releasing a new wineskin for the church, too. One not based on the methods of the past that rely on revival meetings experienced inside the walls of the church, but one that equips people to go out and be the church. Fulfilled and empowered by the Spirit of God. That will happen as individuals experience their own personal transformation.

When everyday believers start cultivating the principles of God's IDEAL in their life, there will be an overflow effect, both in the church and the world. Christians joyfully walking in their identity in Christ, pursuing their unique designs and assignments as led by the Holy Spirit. Committed to each other in good times and bad. Passionate to help and heal the broken, restoring each other back to wholeness, then turning to do the same for others. In homes, coffee shops, art studios and businesses—on front porches and in back yards. Led by leaders who love God and people more than building their political or influential platforms. That's Kingdom!

Recently while worshipping the Lord, I had a vision. I saw a man standing on the porch ringing an old-timey dinner bell. He was ringing the bell intensely, but people were walking by as if they didn't even hear it. Some looked, but they just kept walking. I asked the Lord what that was about and I felt like He said, "That's the church. They stand on the porch, ring the dinner bell and expect everyone to come running, but they're not coming. And those passing by? People once made them promises that never came to pass and now, they don't trust the bell ringers."

*The Gospel of the Kingdom is a "go-and-tell" gospel, not just "come and see"*

Then the scene changed and I saw people walking in groups of two or three out into the community. Each group was carrying unique gifts—like a jug of water, healing balms, etc. As they went along, they ministered to people and then together, they continued on to others. They took what was needed to the people instead of expecting them to come and get it on their own. People were changed and the church grew exponentially. That's what can happen when God's children start walking in God's IDEAL.

The Gospel of the Kingdom is a "go-and-tell" gospel, not just "come and see". On the one hand, the church has defaulted to praying for revival and expecting God to draw people to Sunday meetings supernaturally, or on the other hand, trying to convince people to attend church through slick marketing campaigns and programs on the other. They pray for God to move as He did in the past or market their way to church growth rather than hosting His presence and equipping their people to be carriers of revival and ambassadors of the Kingdom every day.

Unfortunately, this has created fickle spectators with both a consumer mentality and those with a distaste for the modern church. Believers who seek prophetic words and goosebump-encounters in church meetings rather than becoming mature children of God that walk in their design and release the power of the Kingdom. Tired of the show, many believers are disengaging from church altogether. And non-believers see little connection between the modern church and the life of Jesus.

People are done with church as usual. And who can blame them? For generations Christians have been told, "revival is on the way",

"God is about to do this or that", or to "Just hold on". In many places, worship has turned into a religious ritual void of God's power and presence—or extended times of asking God to "come down", "send the glory" and "revive us again" rather than a focus on who God is and what He's already done for us in the New Covenant. Believers living on a roller coaster of well-meaning spiritual hype. And what's the result? Burnout, boredom and a disillusioned heartsick church. But that's what happens when you train generations of church goers to obey the rules, stay in line and don't rock the boat rather than equipping them for the unique assignment to which they've been called. Busy with church work rather than walking in the things God created for them, they become disheartened and desperate for something real. They leave the church and look elsewhere for what only God can give them.

I asked the Lord about my vision of the ringing dinner bell and heard the word "mobilize"—like a military unit preparing for active service. I believe this is the church's job at this hour: to equip each person to operate in their unique design and pursue their unique assignment, so they can release the power of the Kingdom wherever they go with signs and wonders following. As each believer does that in the context of healthy Kingdom community, lives will be changed, cities will be transformed, the church will grow and Jesus will be glorified. That's the fruit of God's IDEAL.

In recent history, many of the major revivals I know of ended with the host churches worse off than before. Leadership struggles. Burned out volunteers. And afterwards, dwindling attendance. And consider the mass crusade movement of the last 100 years. After bringing millions of people to Jesus—praise God—the crusade leaves town and new believers struggle to walk in the reality of the Kingdom that is now theirs. Why? Because they are not discipled. This is not an accusation or indictment, but an honest observation. Momentary encounters are transformative and necessary. We need mountaintop, burning-bush experiences with the Lord throughout our journey. They revive and inspire us all. But if people aren't taught how to take what they've experienced into their practical everyday lives, they end up chasing spiritual experiences rather than living from the Kingdom. There is so much more!

I believe God wants to move in a fresh way, a way that will be marked as much by practical equipping and discipleship as it is by His presence. A revival of Kingdom reality in the life of every believer. A revival of God-focused worship and intimacy with Jesus—of hearing God's voice and walking by faith. Established in His presence, bathed in the Glory of God and filled with supernatural encounters with Him. Worship services filled with healing, salvation and a tangible reality of His overwhelming presence. Believers—demonstrating the reality of the Kingdom in the streets.

I also believe He wants to move through the establishment and nurture of relationships that go beyond Sunday morning. People encouraging and challenging each other to walk in the fullness of their design and assignment. The church as a healthy, living organism that looks like a family, not another hierarchical religious organization based on function.

This is what I believe is on God's heart in this hour: God's children living from the power of the Kingdom that is already living inside them. I am full of faith and hope for all God has promised—because of what He's already done. I want to help usher in this new model of Kingdom living, rooted in discipleship, bathed in the glory of His presence. That's the heart behind God's IDEAL. When individual believers are transformed, so too will the church. Equipped and mobilized to see His Kingdom come on earth as it is in Heaven.

And if you're reading this right now, realizing you've never asked Jesus to come into your heart to be your Lord and Savior, you can take that life-changing step right now. Just pray this simple prayer with me right now as you surrender your life to Christ: *"Father, I confess I am a sinner, and I'm tired of living life on my own. I'm sorry. I believe you sent your son, Jesus, to die on the cross and rise from the dead so that I could be saved. Jesus, I ask you to forgive me of my sins. Come into my heart and make me a new creation. I surrender my life to you wholly and completely. I accept your free gift of salvation now by faith and make you my Lord and Savior. Thank you for this gift of salvation! Fill me now with your Holy Spirit so I can walk in everything you have planned for me; I pray in Jesus' name, amen."*

Now that you understand the basics of ideal living and its potential impact on the wider body of Christ, let's dive deeper into each principle. In the following chapters, I'll show you how to implement each one into your life so you can confidently walk in everything God has designed for you and become a carrier of Kingdom transformation.

# Chapter 3

*The Foundation of Identity in Christ*

In Matthew 7:24-27, Jesus shares the Parable of the Wise and Foolish Builders. He contrasts those who did and did not put His words into practice as wise and foolish. The wise builder built their house on a solid foundation, the foolish one, on shifting sand. In the same way, a healthy identity in Christ is the firm foundation for thriving in the Kingdom of God. And that's more than just the act of being saved. It's knowing and believing who we are in Christ and all that the cross makes available to us once we are saved. Without operating in a healthy identity, everything in life is built on the shifting sands of our feelings, experiences, the opinion of others and the fickle results of our performance—instead of living rooted and grounded in the confident Love of God. Ask me how I know. You guessed it: years of trial, error, pain and frustration.

## Misplaced Identity

For most of my life, I had no idea that it was God's job as my heavenly Father to define me. Consequently, the enemy started early on to distort my identity in Christ. Just like God has an ideal for us, so does the enemy. And it's to steal, kill and destroy everything God has promised you.

I was a sensitive, artsy kid who loved God but had a really challenging relationship with my dad. Everyone in my family loved Jesus the best way we knew how, but we also carried some significant baggage. Suffice it to say, we fought a lot. My parents fought a lot, I fought with my dad a lot and everyone's brokenness was on full display. It made for a few very difficult years growing up. Add to that the significant loss of my grandfather and my piano teacher, sexual abuse by a same-sex family member and you have a recipe for a very wounded, confused young man.

Instead of my earthly father modeling God's design—God intended all fathers to model and imprint the Love of God in our lives—I performed for approval, compared myself to others and felt significant shame about my self-worth. Instead of finding refuge and strength in my relationship with God, I turned church ministry into an opportunity to gain approval through my performance. Instead of walking in healthy relationships, I learned to manipulate and control people and situations to protect myself, hide my perceived weaknesses and mask my pain. Not exactly the picture of healthy Kingdom living, but I could function like that inside a performance-based church culture for many years.

Thankfully, I've received healing and restoration in many areas of my life and extend healing opportunities to others. But back then, those experiences created a lens through which I saw the world that had very little to do with God's best for my life. And that was exactly the enemy's plan: to distort my understanding of who God says I am.

## Distortion & Seduction

If the enemy can distort or destroy our understanding of who we really are in Christ, then everything we build our life on will be built on a faulty foundation. And the lens through which we see ourselves, others, life and God will create a perspective that has nothing to do with God's best for our life in His Kingdom. Without a Christ-centered perspective, life may look good for a little while and you may even function successfully for a season but eventually, the foundation of your life will rot away, leaving you ripe for defeat, destruction and disillusionment. That's what happened in my life until I started learning how the Kingdom worked.

That is why worship, combined with renewing our minds is so powerful. It focuses our attention on Jesus rather than our feelings, perspective, or situation. We begin to see life through the lens of His Word, enlivened by His Spirit rather than through the wounded lens of our experience and false expectations plagued by fear. When we worship and view the world through a Christ-centered perspective, we can walk with confidence in the promises of God rather than the frustrations and defeats of the past.

One of the seductive plots of the enemy is to take an area of weakness, vulnerability, or sin in your life and try to convince you that is who you are. It's much easier to come into agreement with a long-held struggle than measure it against the Word of God, let it be healed and walk in a new reality. There is comfort and familiarity with the old way of living.

Following the seductive plan of the enemy often feels natural, liberating and even empowering for a while. And sadly, there will be

*God's Word
reveals the lies of the
enemy that have become
a part of your normal
way of living.*

many who will cheer you on this alluring new path. But God's Word is clear: "*There is a way that seems right to a man but in the end, it leads only to death.*" Proverbs 14:12 NIV.

No matter what you feel about who you are, always measure what defines you against God's Word. Otherwise, you will be easily deceived. Remember, deception is deceptive! In other words, it happens without you noticing it's happening until it's too late.

God's Word reveals the lies of the enemy that have become a part of your normal way of living. His Word offers you a vision for new life in Christ and is never intended to shame you but to draw you to Himself and offer you a way of escape. He wants to pour the oil of healing on your wounds. It's only in the context of His Word and His presence that will you find true identity.

## Jesus's Identity was Attacked

Matthew 4:1-11 shares the story of Jesus' temptation in the wilderness. This attack immediately followed Jesus' baptism by John the Baptist and the public affirmation by the Father as His Son in whom He was well pleased. A monumental moment for sure in Jesus' earthly life. Imagine the voice of God booming from the clouds declaring for everyone to hear that you are loved, approved and chosen. His identity was being established by the Father—He was who God said He was—His son. This affirmation from the Father was not based on his performance in ministry—He hadn't done anything in ministry yet to speak of. It was based solely on who He was, His identity. This may have been Jesus' greatest moment of affirmation to date.

Riding high on the emotion of this stellar moment, Jesus was then led into the wilderness and tempted by Satan three times in three specific ways: provision, performance and power. Here's the story in Matthew 4:1-11 NLT:

> *"Then Jesus was led by the Spirit into the wilderness to be tempted there by the devil. For forty days and forty nights He fasted and became very hungry. During that time the devil came and said to Him, "If you are the Son of God, tell these stones to become loaves of bread." But Jesus told him, "No! The Scriptures say, 'People do not live by bread alone, but by every word that comes from the mouth of God.'" Then the devil took Him to the holy city, Jerusalem, to the highest point of the Temple, and said, "If you are the Son of God, jump off! For the Scriptures say, 'He will order His angels to protect you. And they will hold you up with their hands so you won't even hurt your foot on a stone.'" Jesus responded, "The Scriptures also say, 'You must not test the Lord your God.'" Next the devil took Him to the peak of a very high mountain and showed Him all the kingdoms of the world and their glory. "I will give it all to you," he said, "if you will kneel down and worship me." "Get out of here, Satan," Jesus told him. "For the Scriptures say, 'You must worship the Lord your God and serve only Him.'" Then the devil went away, and angels came and took care of Jesus."*

Satan still uses the same identity trifecta to tempt us today: provision, performance and power. Through this gauntlet of temptation, He calls God's faithfulness and our identity in Christ into question by asking us similar questions when we are most vulnerable. If God promised us blessings, where are they? Did God really say that? Is He really that good? Does He really have our best at heart? Satan then heaps fear and doubt upon us related to our physical provision—causing worry, stress and striving around money and resources. He tempts us to take things into our own hands rather than trusting the faithfulness of God to provide abundantly for our every need. Then, when that doesn't work, He tempts us to perform and tries to convince us that this journey is all about what we achieve and how others perceive us. Lastly, when those don't work, He promises us the power to change our life rather than trusting in God. His tactics are designed to keep us continually doubting God.

## The Enemy's Plan is Isolation

When the enemy attacks us in the area of our identity, his primary strategy is to convince us we're the only person who's dealing with this particular struggle. And just like in the story of Jesus' wilderness temptation, Satan waits for a vulnerable moment to isolate and overwhelm us. Thankfully, God's Word provides us with many examples of how others throughout generations have dealt with the enemy. Some overcame and some were overcome.

*Jesus overcame the temptations of the enemy by standing firm in His identity as God's Son.*

He knew what His Father thought about Him. He knew He didn't have to prove anything to the devil because His identity was secure. His provision was abundant. Performing for applause wasn't necessary. And ultimately, His power for living came from the Father. He declared God's Word as truth in the face of the enemy's tempting lies. As Jesus came into agreement with God's Word and the Father's heart, He tapped into the grace to overcome the temptations He faced. He resisted the devil; He overcame and the devil fled the scene. What a beautiful model for us!

Although that's the ideal, that's not always how it happens. People often make different choices with different consequences. Consider Adam and Eve. Created by God in perfection, they had everything they needed to thrive and function in the place God had given them. They had all the ideas and opportunities, resources, relationships and authority to do what God put on their heart to do. And, as the icing on the cake, they walked with God each day in intimate fellowship. That's what I would call, ideal. So, what happened? The enemy attacked their identity and they responded in an all-to-common manner, resulting in far-reaching consequences for all humanity.

Satan lied to them about who God was and what He had said, including the possibilities for their life. Just like in the story of Jesus' temptation, he called into question God's willingness to faithfully provide for them. Seeds of doubt, confusion and unbelief were sown. Instead of staying in agreement with God about who they were created to be, who He is and what He said was possible; they came into agreement with the lies of the enemy. And, anytime you come into agreement with something, you give it both opportunity and authority to function in your life. That's awesome when you come into agreement with God, His Word and His purposes for your life. It's disastrous when you come into agreement with the enemy and his lies.

Unfortunately, Adam and Eve's agreement with the enemy caused them to sin, which separated them from God and brought upon them (and us) the curse of having to do life outside of a Kingdom reality. An existence outside of God's abundance meant having to work in the power of their own strength and by the sweat of their brow to provide for their own needs.

Think about that story. The enemy didn't come in with a huge army and capture the Garden of Eden. He didn't physically hold them captive and force them to do anything. He simply sowed doubt into their hearts about God and who He said they were. The rest took care of itself.

Satan uses the same strategy today. But since we know how he works—we can intentionally cultivate a healthy identity in Christ that recognizes the lies before they take root. So how do you establish a healthy identity in Christ? I'm going to show you, but first I want to tell you a story.

# Chapter 4

*The Great Restoration*

Imagine saving all your life for the most fantastic vacation you could imagine. You scrimped and saved—cashed in every coupon, discount and freebie available to you. You budgeted your travel to and from the resort location down to the penny. Once there, you unpack, sit on the balcony and from a bird's eye view overlook the whole resort. It's absolutely incredible. Swimming pools, tennis courts, white sandy beaches, staff standing by to attend to the peoples every need, restaurants boasting offers of the most delicious food and entertainment beyond your wildest imagination. It's a literal cornucopia of opportunity and enjoyment.

Sitting there, you imagine what fun the others are having, what the restaurants are like and what it would be like to lay on the beach enjoying the sun. You feel the warm wind on your skin and hear the laughter of others enjoying themselves on vacation. It's a magical wonderland. Wow, you made it!

Day after day, you walk out onto the balcony and watch the sights and sounds below. As you eat the bologna sandwiches and snacks you meticulously packed (to save money) you imagine what the fresh seafood being delivered to the resort kitchens would taste like after a day of swimming in the ocean and laying on the beach. Day after day you continue this observation until finally, your seven days in paradise are up.

As you check out of the resort, the hotel concierge inquires if you had a nice time and if everything was to your liking? He mentions that he hadn't seen much of you during your seven days stay. In fact, he's only seen you on your balcony.

You reply everything was just fine. You really enjoyed your room but since your budget was tight and everything was so expensive, you brought your own food. But yes, everything had been great!

Puzzled, the concierge asks if you realized you had booked seven days at an all-inclusive resort. He becomes even more puzzled when you reply with a yes and tell him again you enjoyed your room very much! With a consoling look, the concierge puts his hand on your shoulder and explains that all-inclusive meant everything they offered at the resort had already been paid for, including all the food and drinks you could have wanted. You had 24/7 access to all their amenities and the attention of all their staff to make your stay with them as delightful as possible. And then it sinks in. You hadn't taken advantage of any of the resort's benefits. The whole time you were there everything had already been paid for—in full. All you had to do was simply enjoy them.

## Living Below the Promise

Now, that might seem like a fantastical story, but that's how most Christians live their lives. They live well below the promised reality of God's Word simply because they don't know how to access it or that it's even theirs to begin with. Struggling to make it through this life when all the while, everything they need to not just survive, but thrive in every area of life has already been provided for them in abundance; no scrimping, saving or striving required. For most believers, that's as foreign a reality as was the all-inclusive vacation to the man in our story. And yet, it's not just a story. It's their life. It was my life and maybe it's yours right now.

Growing up, I was inadvertently taught many things about how life worked, especially as a Christian. Like most people, I was taught things like "humility means never being concerned about yourself" and "it's better to wait to be asked than ask for what you really want." When it came to making a living, I learned if I worked hard and got a good job, everything would work out. And I learned adages like "money doesn't grow on trees" and "nothing comes easy in this life." And it seemed everyone in church was concerned about being seen as greedy if their car was too new, house was too nice or clothes were too fancy. Consequently, I interpreted thoughts about money through the belief it was more spiritual to be poor—only unspiritual people wanted money. I should keep my eyes focused on God and He would bring me what I needed at the right time (if I obeyed the rules). I never saw very many happy, fulfilled, or thriving Christians. After all, serving God was rarely enjoyable—consider the suffering missionary who left everything to follow Jesus but barely had enough to survive and seemed always in need. Again, that told me God paid poorly, if at all. These unintentional idioms echoed in my subconscious for years without me even realizing they were there.

Once I entered vocational ministry, the mentality of many church people I worked for echoed the old adage, "Lord, you keep him humble and we'll keep him poor" as if poverty, lack and false humility were desirable qualities of a highly spiritual person. I remember one night in particular. My wife shared with me an encounter she had with a woman in the parking lot of our local church. We were newly married. Tanya was a first-year teacher and I was serving as the youth pastor. Since both of us had driven older, unreliable cars during college, we purchased Tanya a new vehicle since she had a long commute to Atlanta daily.

If you've been in church for very long, I bet you can already tell where this is going. As Tanya walked to her car, the woman commented how nice her new car was. Tanya smiled and said thank you. The woman then continued, surmising how the church must be paying her husband a lot of money since it looked like a very expensive car. Stunned and angry, Tanya got in the car and drove home. I wish that was the only encounter we've ever had with church people firing snide drive-by comments, but sadly, it is not.

I got saved because I didn't want to go to hell, not because of the promise of abundant life that Jesus promised. It was pretty much, get saved, don't have anything to do with anything "worldly" (definitions varied depending on the denomination or movement I was involved with)—then hang on until Jesus returns.

I lived most of my Christian life like that. Frustrated, defeated and trying my best to please the Lord, despite my own failures. When I was performing well, everything was great. But when I missed the mark in some way, everything would come crashing down because somehow, I'd let the Lord down. It was a constant emotional and spiritual roller coaster. I spent countless hours repenting, trying to get back on God's good side only to find myself back there time and again. Of course, the enemy exploited those times and over the years it led me into a downward spiral of addiction, depression, performance-orientation and feelings of religious hypocrisy.

## A Lightbulb Moment

Back in the early 2000's, I was on church staff as the Worship Pastor and had a conversation with someone who's now one of my primary mentors and spiritual confidants. To be honest, I was tired of church and over the endless sermons exhorting us to pursue the Lord's presence a little more intensely because revival was just around the corner. I loved God's presence. I loved worshipping and leading others in worship but honestly, it seemed so contrived.

As I expressed my dissatisfaction with my friend, she told me something profound. She looked me in the eyes, smiled and said (and I'm paraphrasing to the best of my memory after all these years), "Matt, you can have as much of the Lord as you want at any time because His Kingdom is living inside of you right now in all its fullness." As she spoke those words, I believed them – I mean, I really grabbed hold of them in my heart – and a lightbulb came on in my spirit. It was as if a veil lifted and I could clearly see for the first time. It wasn't about striving, working for God or performing to please Him. It was about coming into agreement with what was already living inside me through the Kingdom and the power of the Holy Spirit. Wow! From that moment on, my perspective started to shift, though it didn't happen overnight. God brought many Bible teachers, anointed friends, circumstances and revelations my way over the years to bring me into deeper levels of maturity. But as I aligned myself with the truth of His Kingdom, my life completely changed.

If you're thinking you would love to experience that kind of change in your life, too, then keep reading because that's what this book is all about. It's a simple roadmap for stepping into the life you've always dreamed about in the Kingdom, but never knew how to experience—until now.

## Kingdom Alignment

You see, when most people get saved, they are never taught how to actually come into alignment with the truth of God's Word or how to live the abundant life and actually thrive. In fact, most teaching around this topic wildly swings from requiring outward displays of self-righteous religious works and superficial pursuits of holiness (limitations on clothing, hair, makeup, music, etc.) to pursuing hyper-spirituality with no regard to a practical day to day life. We are told to simply stay in God's presence 24/7 through focused prayer, worship and study. Although often sincere, both extremes are based in striving for approval and earning God's Love, a fundamental misunderstanding of how the Kingdom of God works. God's Kingdom works as we co-labor with the Holy Spirit in alignment with our unique design and assignment.

It's quite the conundrum. On one hand we're taught salvation through Jesus is a gift of grace received by faith. Then, as soon as we're "in", we'd better get busy working for the Lord to earn God's approval! I've seen that mentality paralyze or create such a striving spirit within many committed Christians that they burn out: unable

*Being redeemed,
reconciled and restored
means you're back
in the original state
God intended
for you to live in
before sin
entered the picture.*

to hear God's voice, align with their design or be led by the Holy Spirit in their unique assignment. What's a person to do?

## Reality Check

The good news of the Gospel means that even though our sin separated us from God, Jesus came to fully redeem us - from death, hell and the grave. Christ reconciled us back into the relationship with the Father that He had always intended for us and restored us back into our place in His Kingdom as His children—just as if we never sinned. As demonstrated in the story of the Prodigal Son, even though we tried to make it on our own, God in His mercy ran after us and restored all the enemy had stolen. All we must do is simply receive Jesus' gift by faith. Thank you, Lord!

So, what does this restoration really mean? For many Christians, it simply means that by God's mercy, they barely make it into the Kingdom and avoid hell. Some even use the terminology, "I'm just an old sinner saved by God's grace" and others refer to themselves as "just a worm"—all terms to make them appear humble and excuse themselves from personal responsibility. How sad and yes, how completely unbiblical!

Restoration means; being brought back to your original state. You've been reinstated. Are you getting this? Being redeemed, reconciled and restored means you're back in the original state God intended for you to live in before sin entered the picture.

This means when you accepted Jesus into your heart as Lord and Savior, God instantly and permanently restored you. At the cross, Jesus accomplished for you what you could never accomplish for yourself. And the reality of that restoration includes the fact He's given you every right, privilege, resource, relationship and opportunity needed to complete your assignment here on the earth while experiencing the abundant life He promised. This is the beauty of the New Covenant we now have the opportunity walk in. It's really good news.

**Embracing Your Kingdom Identity**

It's important to realize Jesus' finished work on the cross fully restored us to the Kingdom. But for us to experience that restoration in our lives, we must be intentional about what we set our mind on. The internal framework of our heart and mind sets the stage for what we experience in our external reality. That's why renewing our mind is so important. The Bible teaches in Romans 12:2 that transformation occurs, *through* the renewing of our mind. *"Do not be conformed any longer to the pattern of this world but be transformed by the renewing of your mind."* (NIV) In other words,

*If we want to see*
*real transformation in our lives,*
*we have to change the way*
*we think.*

Every child learns to live life through modeling others and through personal experience. Some see the loving smile of their mother and mirror that back to her. They hear the words of their father and try to repeat them, eventually learning language and communication. They feel love and care from those around them, giving them a sense of security and belonging. Unfortunately, many others have the opposite experience as children or adults, leading to opposite results. Instead of feeling safe and secure, they feel inadequate and fearful. Negative coping mechanisms develop which reinforce unhealthy thoughts and over time, their life looks nothing like God's best design. They operate from a broken framework.

Thankfully, Jesus' finished work on the cross can change all that. Instead of living life according to a broken internal framework, we can renew our mind according to the truth of God's Word. As we do, our brain forms new pathways in alignment with the Kingdom of God and fundamentally shifts the way we see and experience the world around us. As our thinking is transformed, our beliefs, habits and actions change too. Although this is a supernatural process, it's something the Holy Spirit does with us, not to us.

## Set Your Mind

In Romans 8:5, Paul reminds us that *"those who live according to the Spirit set their minds on the things of the Spirit."* (NIV) Again, intentionality is required. Why? Because our minds get hardwired from a very early age to see and interpret life through the lens of our experience and beliefs. And rarely does that lens agree with God's best. Most of the time, it magnifies fear, doubt and unbelief: about ourselves, others, God and what's possible. It's a distorted view that leads us down a crooked path to an undesirable destination.

God designed our heart and mind to co-labor with the Holy Spirit in our transformation. Remember, when you were saved, your spirit was instantly transformed. According to scripture, you became a new creation in Christ. 2 Corinthians 5:17 NKJV says, "*Therefore, if anyone is in Christ, He is a new creation; old things have passed away; behold, all things have become new.*" And at the same time, you entered a lifelong journey with the Holy Spirit to transform your thoughts, beliefs, emotions and actions into alignment with the will of God. That process of alignment is both enabled and accelerated through the renewing of your mind. It includes making choices to put off the "old man", giving it no provision—nothing that would enable it to live and thrive—and as Paul said in Romans 13:14 NKJV, to "*...put on the Lord Jesus Christ, and make no provision for the flesh, to fulfill its lusts.*" It's a divine exchange. My thoughts for the mind of Christ. My ways—which may seem right but lead to death—in exchange for His ways that lead to life.

## Saved but Not Satisfied

Without a renewed mind, we are unable to experience the fullness of the New Covenant because we see life through a distorted lens. Our minds continue to walk in defeat, struggle and confusion even though we love Jesus and desire to experience a Spirit-led life. Saved but living out of religious obedience and obligation—void of any real Spirit-led power.

We must renew our mind so we can see ourselves, our life and God through the lens of what's possible in the Kingdom. When we see things the way God intended, faith grows toward a new Kingdom vision and our beliefs and actions will be inspired, shaped and fueled by the Kingdom of God.

## How Renewing Your Mind Works

Renewing our minds is not just a spiritual process, but a physiological one as well. Through the research of many neuroscientists, we now know that when we intentionally align our thoughts with God's Word, it creates new connections and pathways in our brain through the process of neuroplasticity. These new pathways assist us by creating personalized solutions, strategies and opportunities for our lives that best align with God's plan. And, the process of renewing our minds becomes easier. Over time, we begin to prefer this way of thinking with God. Amazing.

If we want to experience a different life – the abundant life Jesus promised – we must learn to intentionally renew our minds. Remember, in Proverbs 23:7 KJV it says, *"For as he thinketh in his heart, so is he."* In other words,

*The thoughts you dwell on create the world you dwell in.*

Renewing your mind according to God's Word is an ongoing process of healing. Through it, the Holy Spirit unlocks the prison doors of fear, anxiety and unworthiness, allowing us to walk free. We are reintroduced to God's truth and restored to love. As we intentionally pursue the renewing of our mind, He releases His transforming power within us and we experience change. As we are set free, our life and work reflect that freedom, becoming an invitation for others to step into this new reality. It's a beautiful thing.

## The 5R's for Renewing Your Mind

How does renewing of the mind happen practically? Well, volumes have been written about renewing the mind, but I hope I can simplify the process for you with something I call the 5R's: Recognize, Repent, Replace, Reinforce and Rejoice.

### Recognize

The first step is to recognize whether the thoughts you are thinking align with the truth of God's Word or with the lies of the enemy. This requires daily intimacy with Jesus: getting into His presence, learning to hear His voice and responding to the leading of the Holy Spirit. Doing so increases your awareness of what's true and what's not.

When learning to recognize both God's truth or the enemy's lie, we need to "*take every thought captive*" as the Bible says in 2 Corinthians 10:5. That simply means to stop and examine the thought, compare it against the Word of God and see it from God's perspective. Does it align with God's Word or align with a negative belief, expectation, or experience? Does this thought sound like the voice of Jesus or the accuser, leading me into life or death? Though this requires intentionality, it's a quick way to determine the source of our thoughts.

When Paul encourages believers in Romans 13 to make no provision for the flesh and all the lust that comes with it, he's essentially saying we are not to give our old nature room to operate. Don't give it any air or attention. If we do, it will continue to flourish, leading us in directions we don't want to go and produce results we don't want to experience.

## Repent

The next step is to repent. If after examining a thought (or thought pattern), you realize you have been believing a lie from the enemy and it's become a normal part of your world view—repent. In the Bible, the word for repent means to "change your mind". When you do, you come out of agreement with the lie and close the door to the enemy—denying him the opportunity to use that lie in your life. That's powerful. When we repent; we declare our decision to go in a different direction and ask God to forgive us for trusting in something other than Him because we believed something about Him that wasn't true.

## Replace

Now that you've recognized and repented, replacing those thoughts with the truth of God's Word is essential. It can be as simple as asking the Holy Spirit to bring to your remembrance a scripture that is opposite of the lie you may be faced with. You can also do a quick internet search for scripture verses based on the lie you're trying to replace. Remember, our thoughts are like seeds. Whatever we plant in the garden of our hearts will bring forth a harvest. So, choose your seeds wisely. If you don't like the harvest you're seeing in your life, change the seeds you're planting. Replace your thought.

# Reinforce

Since every action begins with a thought, renewing our minds make it more likely our actions are originating from the mind of Christ rather than the mind of our flesh. Doing this over time builds confidence. And that brings us to the next of the 5R's: Reinforce. Remember, Jesus said in Matthew 6:24, we can't serve two masters. Setting our mind on the truth of God's Word and responding in obedience are the primary ways we establish Christ as Master of our life.

The promises of God become weapons in our hands when we learn how to use them. Every time you are flooded with thoughts that disagree with God's best for your life, simply reject and replace them with God's Word. One way you can accelerate this process is to create and write down Biblical affirmations. I suggest writing them on note cards and laminating them so you can carry them with you for easy access. You can also post them in places where you will see them: like your office wall, your desk, your car or even your bathroom mirror. Keep them on your computer desktop or even on your mobile device like I do. This can feel tedious at first, but as you do so with gratitude, faith and expectancy, God's presence will infuse the process, making it become more and more natural.

I have found it also helps to use our imagination in this process. God created us with the ability to see, sense, feel and create new realities in our minds before they ever come into the physical realm. It's one of the primary ways we co-labor with the Holy Spirit to release His Kingdom in and through our lives. As you begin to recognize, replace and reinforce your thoughts based on God's Word, imagine in your mind's eye what it would look and feel like to experience life within this new reality. Invite the Holy Spirit to walk with you in your imagination as you engage all your God-given senses. This will further stimulate your brain and accelerate your ability to come into agreement with God's Kingdom.

## Rejoice

The last part of this renewing your mind process is to rejoice. As a part of your daily time with the Lord, express your gratitude to God for your new Kingdom reality. Thank Him by journaling, using your imagination, or through creative expression—like art, dance and music. As you express your thankfulness for all God has provided to you in the New Covenant, the Holy Spirit will cultivate and reinforce your new internal reality.

As you practice the 5 R's, the lens through which you see life will change. Your mind and life's inner framework will begin to align with the Kingdom of God. And, your identity in Christ will become firmly established in your inner man.

## Walking in Community

Finally, a key part of establishing a healthy identity in Christ is walking in life-giving relationship with other believers. When you cultivate relationships with people that encourage and challenge you to walk in the fullness of your new identity, momentum grows. You weren't designed to live life alone or stand against the schemes of the enemy by yourself. You will be strengthened in community as you invest in others and allow others to invest in you.

God's Word says in Proverbs 11:25 NIV, *"...He who refreshes others will himself be refreshed."* As you intentionally develop community with other believers, take time to speak words of life and blessing over each other. Honor each person's uniqueness. Remind one another of the promises God has spoken to each one. Pray for God-solutions to problems you are facing and create a culture around you of expectation and faith toward the things of the Kingdom.

God's Word also says in James 5:16 NIV, *"Confess your sins to one another and you will be healed."* In other words, as you walk in both encouragement and vulnerability with others in the context of loving Christian community, you will be strengthened, healed and come into maturity. Share your struggles. Ask for help. Honor each other by keeping confidences among the community. As you share both your strengths and struggles, the bonds of friendship will grow strong and you will experience the power of the Kingdom of God. Remember,

*Having your heart and mind transformed into the likeness of Christ is a process that takes a lifetime.*

As you begin this journey, you will have moments of breakthrough and moments of resistance. The moments of resistance may seem overwhelming at first, but realize you have more experience living from a framework that doesn't align with God's best for you than you do with this new normal you're beginning to cultivate. It may seem tedious and uncomfortable at times. But don't give up. His mercies are new every morning. As you commit to the process moment by moment and trust the Spirit of God within you, you will experience His empowering grace and transformation—all from a new Kingdom perspective.

# Chapter 5

*What Does God Say About You?*

Now that you understand the basics of how to establish and cultivate your new identity in Christ, let's take a deeper look at what's promised to us in the Kingdom through the New Covenant. Knowing what God has promised is foundational to renewing our minds. Without it, we are simply hoping in the power of positive thoughts rather than sowing the living Word of God into our lives. Positive thoughts are helpful but sowing the Word of God in our hearts and minds produces eternal fruit.

God always speaks to us from the place of promise and destiny. In Christ, He sees us as He designed and intended, not through the lens of our weakness, sin and old identity. When He speaks, He calls out His purposes for our life and breathes upon those things He put inside of us. Like Gideon in the threshing floor in Judges 6; we often feel inadequate to face the situations we are walking through. But in that very place, God speaks to who we are in Him. He called Gideon a mighty warrior, instead of a scared runaway. He called Abram the father of many nations instead of one who doubted the goodness of God. He called Paul a chosen vessel to bear His name before kings even though he had persecuted the people of God for years. Just like these Biblical heroes, God defines our identity based on His goodness, not our weakness. He sees Christ in you and me, the hope of glory. Not our shortcomings.

## Not Designed to Strive

It was never God's intention for us to try and figure out how to live life on our own. Because of sin and the curse of Adam, we became separated from God and on our own, but that was never God's design. Now, because of the finished work of Jesus, we no longer live life in our own strength. Made one with Christ, we are learning to cooperate with the Holy Spirit so Jesus can live His life through us.

Paul reminds us in Galatians 2 NIV, *"I have been crucified with Christ and I no longer live, but Christ lives in me. The life I now live in the body, I live by faith in the Son of God, who loved me and gave himself for me."* In other words, as we walk by faith, Jesus lives through our unique, God-given design and everything we submit to His Lordship.

## You Already Have All Things

Living by faith is more than just believing Jesus died for our sins so we can go to heaven. That's foundational but it's not everything. It's just the starting point. Living by faith includes laying hold of—with confident expectation—everything God has promised us. Walking according to the truth of His Word. Think about it. What good would it be to know we had been fully restored to the Kingdom as God's child without the ability to walk in the reality of that Kingdom? None! That's why we must renew our minds according to who God is, who He says we are and what He says is available. It shifts and aligns our internal framework to what's possible in the Kingdom for us as God's child.

In 2 Peter 1:3-4 ESV the Bible says, *"His divine power has granted to us all things that pertain to life and godliness, through the knowledge of Him who called us to His own glory and excellence, by which He has granted to us His precious and very great promises, so that through them you may become partakers of the divine nature, having escaped from the corruption that is in the world because of sinful desire."* Think of this reality! Everything you need for life and godliness is already provided through the precious promises of God. In other words, it's through His promises that we receive everything God has promised us—like a huge Kingdom pipeline that delivers to us everything we need, to do what God has called us to do in the Kingdom. And, as we receive all He's promised by faith, we can participate fully in the "divine nature" (or the reality of the Kingdom) without stressing or striving on our own. This is the Great Restoration. That God, in His mercy and by His grace, reinstated us as His children through the finished work of Jesus on the cross. And all we have to do is receive it by faith. That is indeed, good news!

## Refocus Your Mindset

We no longer have to spend our Christian life begging God! Or, continuing to try and manipulate or persuade Him to bless us. Just like Jesus said in Luke 12:32, it's His good pleasure to give us the Kingdom! As we spend time in intimacy with Him and get to know His voice, declare His promises over our lives and sow them as seeds in our hearts, we participate in the fullness of the Kingdom. Understanding what's been made available to us as His children through the Great Restoration gives us the ability to agree and receive these promises by faith. Make sense?

This is why cultivating an awareness of God's presence, knowing His Word and recognizing His voice is foundational for every believer. Otherwise, we'll walk around feeling and acting like an orphan while having the rights and benefits of being a son. Through faith, we appropriate all of God's precious promises into our lives and live in the reality they offer. That means when we see a promise in God's Word, all we need to do is agree it's ours in Christ, receive it by faith and then take Spirit-led action to see it become our reality. That is really good news!

## Agreement with God

It should now be clear that everything God calls us to do in His Kingdom happens as the result of our agreement with who He says we are and what He says we can have, do and experience. Thankfully, we don't have to guess what those things are because they have been revealed in God's Word. Our agreement with God's Word opens the door for His promises to flow abundantly into our lives. It's like opening a door in the spirit and saying, "Come on in!"

For just a moment, imagine the spiritual reality Peter is talking about in 2 Peter 1:3-4. Before time began, God already prepared everything His children would need to thrive in every area of our life. And even though Adam and Eve walked away from it in the Garden, Jesus fully restored it to us when He redeemed and reconciled us to the Father. Everything we need already exists in the Kingdom. I don't know if it's in a big heavenly storehouse with your name on it, floating around in the realm of the Spirit, or existing somewhere in the heart of God, but I know it's been restored to you. That's amazing.

*Don't let past experiences of lack distort your vision of what's possible with God.*

## Faith is Like a Bridge

Faith is the process through which we receive everything in God's Kingdom. The bridge we walk across to appropriate everything you need to thrive in this life. As we learn to see and agree with Heaven, those things that exist in the realm of the spirit begin to supernaturally show up in our lives here on earth, the fruit of our agreement with God's promises. That's how faith works—we see and agree.

Recently in a dream, the Lord spoke to me about faith. In the dream, I saw a large machine with a conveyor belt. As I used the levers on the machine, everything I needed came right to me. It was awesome! He was encouraging me to use the tools He's designed for both my benefit and His Glory.

Now I know for some, that might be a stretch based on what you've always been taught. But remember, when we pray, we are to pray believing everything we're asking for is already ours. Jesus said that, not me. Jesus said that when we pray and believe, we can have anything we ask for when we ask for it 'in His name'.

Don't let past experiences of lack distort your vision of what's possible with God. In the Kingdom, things are given by God's grace and appropriated by our faith. Everything is possible through faith because faith brings us into agreement with what God has already purposed, given and established.

## Seeing is Believing

You may be thinking, "But, I thought Romans 10:17 said that "Faith comes by hearing and hearing through the Word of God?" Where does seeing come into play?" The word for "hearing" in the scripture above is *akoēs* which refers to inner or spiritual hearing. And the word used for "word" in the last part of that scripture is *rhéma* which refers to the spoken word, rather than the written word. While faith does grow in our hearts as we read God's Word, the implication in this verse in Romans is that faith comes through learning how to hear God's voice through our *spiritual* inner hearing. Why? Because faith is much more than cognitive agreement with sterile, mental concepts. Faith happens in our hearts.

## More than Information

Many Christians today have cerebral knowledge about God. They have information. They know the stories of Jesus. And, they pursue the principles Jesus taught as faithfully as they can. But unfortunately, many do so without having an ongoing spiritual encounter with Jesus. One where His voice is actively speaking to their heart and they respond in agreement. One where they are enabled by His power, not their own abilities or good intentions.

Without an ongoing intimate encounter with God and dialogue with the Holy Spirit, Christians live without the power of Christ— good people with good intentions. While admirable, that's not what the Kingdom of God is all about. If that were the measuring stick, then there's really no difference between the church and a local civic club in your town that does good things for people all day long.

God's plan for living in the Kingdom is for us to be filled with His power, led by His voice and to release His presence in the world in line with our unique design and assignment. That kind of living brings transformation. And we can't walk like that without faith.

## Fully Convinced

The essence of faith is a heart fully convinced that what God has said is true, even when it doesn't make sense in the natural. So convinced, that we're willing to take steps toward what He's spoken, even though we can't yet see it in the physical realm. And central to being convinced is our imagination. It's one of the beautiful ways we can interpret His voice. When God speaks or reveals something, it's often accompanied by an internal movie, image, sense or feeling. We see what He's saying. Or hear what He's showing us. It's a beautiful, creative mystery that encourages faith to form inside us. It happens as we see and hear with our heart, are led by the Holy Spirit and informed by God's Word.

Once we recognize what God is showing us, we will always have an opportunity to respond. To agree or disagree, welcome or reject. People often disagree with the dreams and visions God gives them out of unbelief caused by fear—causing them to be double-minded and unstable. When we say "yes" to what He shows us, the Spirit will help us take steps in that direction.

Faith is more than belief alone. The Bible says in James 2:17 that, *"Faith without works is dead."* Faith always requires action. It is your active response to what God has said. Remember the time the disciples were out fishing all night in John 21? They had done everything they knew how to do in the natural. They probably went to their favorite fishing hole, used their best bait and even made sure to use their lucky nets. But still, nothing. Then Jesus came on the scene. He told them to throw their nets on the right side of the boat and that they would find some there. He didn't say they might find some. He told them what would work in that specific situation at that specific time. That's how things work in God's Kingdom.

Can you imagine the look on the disciple's faces when they heard Jesus? I'm sure they were like, "Ok, whatever!" But they believed Jesus even though it made no sense in the natural. And the results were astonishing. The Bible says they were unable to haul in the net because of the overwhelming number of fish they caught. Think of that! A little bit of faith in Jesus at the right time caused a huge harvest in their life. The same can be true for you, too.

Do you need a business idea or strategic connection in the marketplace? Financial provision or a roof over your head? How about insight into how to handle a situation at home or work? Remember, everything has already been provided to you in the Kingdom. All you have to do is ask for His direction. Listen to His voice. See and agree with God in prayer and then obey in faith—even if it doesn't make sense to your natural mind. Start walking toward the solutions He shows you. Wherever and when Jesus says to throw your net, do it! You never know how many fish might be swimming by your boat at that very moment. That's how supernatural provision happens in God's Kingdom. And it's available to everyone, including you.

## Faith in Action

Several years ago, the Lord led me through a dream to close my art studio and gallery in Asheville's River Art's District. And I gave Him my "yes". I won't go into all the drama that surrounded me when I actually obeyed the Lord in that decision, but it wasn't easy. I had a lot of identity tied up in my success as an artist in that location. But of course, it was the right decision and God's perfect timing. The dream came several months before the COVID pandemic hit.

It took me a few months to gather the courage to tell my landlord of almost ten years we were moving and would not be renewing our lease. Much to my surprise, in the height of the pandemic, my neighbor at the building decided to take over my studio space and expand their business. It turned out to be a smooth and almost immediate transition.

I knew I was supposed to move my studio out but to where? My heart's desire was to have a more private and secluded studio space to create and write, rather than the public studio I had enjoyed for years. And then I also had the challenge of physically preparing to move. I mean, how would I clean out and move everything quickly? This was a 3000 square foot gallery and art studio chock full of supplies, materials, etc. It wasn't going in my garage, that's for sure!

Now I'm not proud about this, but I immediately went into striving and panic mode, doubting my "yes" that I gave to the Lord. Panicked and not knowing what I was going to do, I feverishly started looking for spaces to rent in the area (I'm a recovering striver). Nothing. I thought about constructing a building on our property. No peace. But I still felt desperate. One day, I was so worked up that I asked Tanya to get in the car with me so we could just drive. When she asked me where we were going, I told her I had no idea. I was looking for anything that could work as a studio.

We wasted several hours and a lot of gas scouring the city of Asheville looking for a space and found absolutely nothing. On the way home, frustrated and even more exasperated, I heard the still small voice of the Lord tell me to look at Craigslist one more time. I was driving, so I asked Tanya to pull up Craigslist to see if anything had come up on the rental listings. She did and just started laughing. A new listing had just popped up. It was exactly what I needed and the best part was, it was only 3 minutes from our home in a beautiful, rural setting that overlooked a secluded pasture and had a mountain view.

I immediately called the building owner and set up a meeting for the next day. We met and after a brief conversation and a quick tour, rented the building on the spot. He told me during our meeting that he didn't believe in rent increases. I chuckled to myself thinking how this already sounded like the Lord. He then said he would split the cost of a new HVAC system with me and install a rollup door if I wanted. Plus, he offered not to charge us rent until our buildout was completed. We were once again astounded at the goodness of God. It was exactly what I had asked the Lord for and more than I could imagine. And, right on time. That's how things work in the Kingdom.

When we give God our faith "yes" and walk toward the vision He's given us, He promises to direct our steps—even if we get freaked out along the way. This is His story. God wants to prosper you in everything He's called you to. He is orchestrating your steps and the pace of your journey. Just keep going.

## Your New Reality in Christ

God's Word gives us a wonderful picture of all the Kingdom has to offer us as a restored son and daughter. My goal is to help you recalibrate your heart to this Kingdom reality. As you begin this process of renewing your mind, trust me. Your life will change.

This process requires intentionality on our part. We must choose to daily point our hearts and minds toward God's truth and away from what has been true for us in the past. Our past experiences, feelings and natural inclinations may not align with God's best for us. That's why we have to choose to fix our thoughts on what is true, honorable, right, pure, lovely and admirable and to think about excellent things worthy of praise, as Paul reminds us in Philippians 4:8.

As one who's been redeemed and restored into the fullness of God's Kingdom, you have a new identity in Christ. Who you are is no longer based on your past, your weaknesses or strengths, or even the opinions of others. It's based on what God says about you. To reorient our hearts and minds to our new reality, we must stand on the unchanging truth of God's Word. I suggest looking up each of the scriptures listed below and using them as daily affirmations to reinforce God's truth for your life. And please, resist the urge to skip this exercise by skimming over these scriptures or saying you'll do it later. If you'll take the time to engage, I promise this will be transformational for you.

You are completely accepted as a son & joint heir with Jesus.
* Romans 8:17, Ephesians 1:5-7, Galatians 3:26-29

You have been freed from the guilt, shame and fear of the past.

- Psalm 103:12, John 3:17, Romans 8:1-2, 1 John 1:9

In Christ, everything is now possible for you.

- Matthew 19:26, Luke 1:37, Philippians 4:13, Romans 8:31

## Promises About What You've Been Given

Now that you know who and whose you are, we can talk about what comes to us with this new identity. Remember, God didn't restore us to the Kingdom simply to rescue us from hell. He redeemed, reconciled and restored us to Himself so we could walk in our original God-given design and flow with Him under the leadership of the Holy Spirit as a conduit of His life. To do that, we need supernatural ideas and opportunities, resources and relationships. It's not enough to work for God. In the Kingdom, we work with God in the context of an intimate relationship that honors our design, listens for His voice and daily follows His lead.

Here are some of the things God has given you to be effective and fulfilled as you walk in the Kingdom as His son/ daughter:

You have been healed.

- 3 John 1:2, Isaiah 53:5, James 5:14-15. 1 Peter 2:24

You have been given everything you need for life and godliness.

- Matthew 6:33, 2 Peter 1:3-4, Philippians 4:19,
  Matthew 7:11

You have been given authority, power, love and a sound mind.

- Romans 8:11, Ephesians 1:19-21, Ephesians 2:1-6,

Acts 3:6, Philippians 4:13

You have been given abundant financial provision & the ability to create wealth.

- Deuteronomy 8:18, Proverbs 10:22, Isaiah 45:3, Psalm 46:1-3

You can have the desires of your heart.

- Psalm 37:4, Psalm 20:4, Psalm 145:19, John 15:7

You can have strength in adversity.

- Romans 8:28, 1 Peter 5:10, Psalm 46:1-3

You have been given eternal life in Christ.

- John 3:16, Romans 6:23, 1 John 5:11-13

You are surrounded and protected by the host of heaven.

- Exodus 23:20, Psalm 34:7, Hebrews 1:14

## Promises About All You Can Do

When we know who we are in Christ and that we've been given everything we need to co-labor with Him in our God-given assignment, the doing part becomes much easier! It's simply walking by faith with a heart of expectation, knowing that God has already prepared our way. He's in everything He's called us to do and is with us in every place He's called us to go. Agree with who God says you are, receive by faith what He's given you and walk as if the promises are already manifested in your life.

Remember, Jesus taught us to pray as if we've already received what we're asking for, saying in Mark 11:24 ESV, "*I tell you, you can pray for anything, and if you believe that you've received it, it will be yours."* Ours as we walk with confidence, knowing everything in the Kingdom happens as the result of agreeing with God and walking by faith.

You can co-labor with God.
* Genesis 2:19, Romans 4:17-22, 1 Corinthians 3:9

You can walk in the supernatural favor & blessing of God.
* Psalm 5:12, Proverbs 8:35, Deuteronomy 28:2

You can live in rest and cease striving.
* Hebrews 4:9-10, Zechariah 4:6, Isaiah 30:15

You can hear, recognize and respond to God's voice.
* John 10:27, John 14:26, Romans 8:14, Isaiah 30:21

You can operate from a place of encounter, not just information.
* 1 Samuel 16:14-23, John 5:19, John 14:16-17

You can walk in uncommon wisdom, strategy and favor.
* Proverbs 3:5-6, Proverbs 16:9, Jeremiah 33:3, John 14:26

You bring supernatural solutions to world problems.
* Genesis 42, 1 Kings 18:20-40, Esther 4:14

You can release light and the life of God.
* Exodus 9:1, Acts 5:15, Matthew 5:15-16

You can bind the enemy, loose the power of Heaven & set captives free.
* Isaiah 61, Matthew 10:8, Matthew 18:18-20, John 14:12

Can you feel the momentum building? I hope you're starting to get a real clear picture of what's possible for you living inside the Kingdom of God. Trust me, it's a lot more than what we've previously settled for! In the next chapter, we'll keep building as I show you how God uniquely created you to co-create Heaven's reality with Him here on earth.

# Chapter 6

*Uniquely Created*

When God created humanity, He designed us to be image bearers. God wanted people to see a glimpse of Him when they met His children. How beautiful, to be entrusted with such a holy responsibility. But since no one person or part of creation (other than Jesus) could ever bear the full image of God in and through their life, each person received a part of God's nature to reveal and reflect. And as we operate together in the body of Christ, the world gets to see God on display. It's amazing. As Paul said in 1 Corinthians 12:27 NLT, "*All of you together are Christ's body, and each of you is a part of it.*" That's God's design.

As a uniquely created being, you have been designed to see the world differently. That's the second part of God's IDEAL: Design. Because of the unique way we see the world, we respond to and interact differently with the world. Unfortunately, religion and church culture often squelch unique expressions in an effort to create a homogeneous community of people all moving in the same direction. They often want people to look the same and respond in like manner. That strategy may seem to be expedient, but it's certainly not based in God's Word. In fact, it often comes from a desire to manage and control rather than inspire, equip and release God's people for their unique Kingdom role.

*Gifts are the talents
and abilities to perform and
accomplish tasks
in the Kingdom.
Graces are the God-given,
supernatural ability to
function and thrive
in situations where others
would normally
struggle.*

One of my favorite quotes is from the early church father, St. Irenaeus. He said, "The glory of God is man, fully alive."

I've always interpreted that to mean there's no greater way to glorify God than to pursue the Kingdom in the context of our unique design and do the things for which He designed us. The things that really make us come alive. To not embrace your uniqueness is to deny the creative brilliance of God and His opportunity to flow through your life. And trust me. Knowing who God designed you to be is really freeing. It will keep you from trying to be everybody else.

God created you with a unique Kingdom design and deposited within you gifts and graces which allow you to operate in joy, fulfillment and connection with Him. Think of it this way. Your design is the unique lens through which you see the world and reflect His image to the world. It informs your perspective on how you see problems, possibilities and solutions. Combined with a healthy identity in Christ, your design becomes a God-given superpower. Giving you the power to experience and accomplish things you would never be able to by yourself. Gifts are the talents and abilities to perform and accomplish tasks in the Kingdom. Graces are the God-given, supernatural ability to function and thrive in situations where others would normally struggle.

Your God-given design, gifts and graces gives you the innate ability to do certain things without a lot of work, effort, or anxiety. Now that you understand the basics, let's dive into how these three— design, gifts and graces—work together.

## Unique Design

I began recognizing my own uniqueness early in my life. I loved art, music and relished moments where I could perform and be on stage. I had big emotions, highs and lows that seemed to be too much for some people. I loved to dress in nice clothes and paid attention to how I looked. I was often self-conscious of what others thought of me and ended up creating a persona I thought others would love. My mind was always going toward big impact and big dreams—for myself, for God and for the world. When I started working in the ministry, my focus was most often on finding ways to inspire the most people, grow the church and see masses of people impacted for the Kingdom. This just came naturally to me, without trying. Part of the unique package I received when God created me. Even though it would require maturing and growth—I viewed and interacted with the world through a God-given lens.

Through my study of what's commonly known as the Redemptive Gifts, I later realized that God designed me as an Exhorter—the fourth of seven gifts listed in Romans 12. This fourth gift, the Exhorter, is reflected in the fourth day of creation as described in Genesis when God created the sun, moon and stars. In other words, I was designed by God to light up the room, be bright, shiny and inspiring. I was designed to lead the way and gather others toward a vision of what could be.

The more I learned about my unique design, the more I understood that people designed like me viewed the world through a big, global impact lens. We want to touch as many people as possible and gather millions of people into the Kingdom. Exhorters like myself, often have the gifts of teaching, speaking, creativity and engaging with others. We are naturally gifted to gather and grow large groups of people to a vision, along with the grace to do it without becoming overwhelmed.

## Design Uncovered

Once I realized God designed me in this way, it was a gamechanger. It was like I had uncovered a hidden gem. I no longer felt self-conscious about my design or feeling "extra". I could celebrate how God created me to be. But prior to that knowledge, I often felt I had to turn down my volume and operate in a religiously-acceptable false humility in order to not be seen as prideful. Even though I always knew I was created for more because of the passion that had burned in me since I was a young boy. Thankfully, understanding my design changed everything. For the first time in my life, I knew who I was and embraced my design as a gift from God. It also revealed why I struggled in certain areas and flourished in others. Why I got along easily with some people and had difficult encounters with others. Embracing my God-given uniqueness and learning to mature in it helped me more fully understand how God wanted me to bear His image.

As you consider your unique design, you may relate to my story above or one of the myriad characters we see in God's Word. David was designed as an intuitive, sensitive lover of God. He saw the world through relationship, passion and creativity. Nehemiah was designed as a builder with a way of seeing the world that was architectural, structural, restorative. Mary and Martha were both loved by Jesus but one was a worshipper, lover and intuitive responder while the other was an administrative, organizer and doer. Paul was a teacher who loved detailed exposition of the law and the intricacies of theology. Peter was bold, loud and tended to be overzealous, but God used him to bring thousands to Him in just one sermon.

Just like you and me, each of these people were uniquely designed by God to bear His image in the world. Sure, they were a work in progress. But if had they resisted or sought to replace their design with one that seemed to be a better fit, think of what the world would have lost. Think of the stories of God's goodness that might not have been told. Think of the demonstrations of the Kingdom that we would never have seen. Embracing your unique design will bless you personally, but it's also for the benefit of others. So, they can encounter His presence and experience what God is really like through you!

### Gifts & Talents

In addition to our design, God also gives us unique gifts (both spiritual and natural) and talents that help us bear His image in the world. They encourage, build up, bring fulfillment and joy to our lives and the lives of others. Things like music and art are often the first things we think about when someone mentions talents and gifts, but there's so much more, including things like business acumen, administration and kindness. And in I Corinthians 12, the spiritual gifts list includes: words of wisdom, words of knowledge, faith, healing, miracles, prophecy, discernment of spirits, tongues and the interpretation of tongues. Whether you have been given a spiritual gift like discernment or a natural talent like the ability to sing, draw, run, dance, or speak, all gifts and talents require intentional development and maturity.

One of the best examples of how to operate in our God-given gifts is found in Exodus 31:1-5 where the artist, Bezalel, is described in detail during his introduction as the artist who would lead a team of other artisans to construct the Tabernacle of Moses. *"Then the LORD said to Moses, "Look, I have specifically chosen Bezalel son of Uri, grandson of Hur, of the tribe of Judah. I have filled him with the Spirit of God, giving him great wisdom, ability, and expertise in all kinds of crafts. He is a master craftsman, expert in working with gold, silver, and bronze. He is skilled in engraving and mounting gemstones and in carving wood. He is a master at every craft!"* (NLT)

Bezalel was both filled with the spirit of God and skilled in his work as an artist. That's the Kingdom model for how we mature in our gifts: filled and skilled. Otherwise, we are either filled with vision but lack the ability to see it come to fruition. Or conversely, we rely on our own abilities apart from God's empowering Spirit. When we are filled with His Spirit through cultivating His presence while simultaneously growing in the skills we need to flourish, our capacity to release God's transforming light and life enlarges. That's when things get fun!

## Supernatural Grace

God releases supernatural grace to us with our design. I like to think about grace in this sense as the innate ability He gives us to do certain things without much work, effort or anxiety. For example, you may be designed as an administratively gifted person – maybe a

Ruler in Redemptive Gifts language. And as part of that design, you have the gift of discernment. The ability to evaluate people and situations quickly to build structures in the most efficient and effective way possible. Additionally, there may be a grace on your life to work with project planning, details and numbers. When you're in the zone building a project plan, writing a budget and thinking of all the details that need to be included, you're truly in your sweet spot. However, when you put a big picture, fast thinking visionary like me in that same situation, I would curl up in a fetal position and cry out for mercy. Why? Wrong design, wrong gifts, no grace.

However, if your design is a Mercy in redemptive gifts language - intuitive, feeling-oriented person - you may have a special gift of compassion and empathy. God uses this mercy gift to help you connect deeply with others and Himself. But put a black and white, administratively focused person in that same situation and it could very well be a recipe for disaster. Why? It's not that they couldn't function in those situations if they had to, but that's not their sweet spot.

Don't get me wrong. We should be growing in all the attributes of God's nature and displaying the fruits of the Spirit in our life. But at the same time, we can't be all things to all people in every situation. We need each other.

## Maturing in Your Design

No matter how God created us, our design always requires maturity in Christ. And, again, that process requires intentionality. In 2 Peter 1:3-4, Peter told us we've already been given all things. And, *everything we need for life and godliness* comes in the context of our God-given design. But he goes on in verses 5-8 saying, "*For this very reason, make every effort to add to your faith goodness; and to goodness, knowledge; and to knowledge, self-control; and to self-control, perseverance; and to perseverance, godliness; and to godliness, mutual affection; and to mutual affection, love. For if you possess these qualities in increasing measure, they will keep you from being ineffective and unproductive in your knowledge of our Lord Jesus Christ.*" (NIV) In other words, while we have been given everything we need, we must mature in each area to fulfill everything God has planned for your life. It's not enough to just have knowledge about something. We must pursue the wisdom and understanding needed to make that knowledge effective.

We each have areas of our life where we need to grow in maturity. As an exhorter, one of my immature tendencies is to quickly run ahead of God's timing with the ideas He shows me. But my wife is a Ruler by design and a slower, more methodical processor and a little slower to change. However, together we're a great team. As we've learned to mature and walk together in our unique designs, God has used us to envision and build great things with Him in the Kingdom. I have learned to let ideas marinate in His presence and trust godly counsel, while Tanya has learned to be open to new ideas and pursue them in a little faster timeline than she might normally operate.

## Maturing in Your Gifts

The gifts God places in us require an intentional process of maturity. Kind of like when people watch a short video clip of a master craftsmen creating in their studio and think they could easily create something just as beautiful. But that doesn't mean they actually could when given the same materials and timeframe. Why? Because the video made the process look easy but they haven't developed the wisdom and understanding needed to implement such a skill.

I've had countless students tell me they had no idea making a basket was so difficult. Though they knew the technique and had all the materials needed, 2 hours of instruction didn't enable them to create their dream basket. My thirty years of making and growing in my gift made it look easy.

# Knowledge is easy to acquire. It's wisdom and understanding that take time.

God's gifts come to us as seeds, full of potential. We can choose to cultivate the gifts or let them lay dormant. We can also choose how we use them—for our own glory, pleasure and gain—or, for the benefit of the Kingdom in line with our assignment. Some mistakenly think If we don't use our gifts for God's Glory, He takes them away. But the Bible says in Romans 11:29 NKJV, "*For the gifts and the calling of God are irrevocable.*" The gifts God gives you belong to you. How you use them is up to you. Investing in your own growth, under the leadership of the Holy Spirit, honors God. It also expands your capacity to flow with Holy Spirit inspiration.

But you must choose how to grow and use your gifts. The supernatural flow of heaven moves through you as you offer your gifts and talents to the Lord and ask Him to lead you.

Someone once shared this old adage with me, "If the only tool you have in your toolbelt is a hammer, then every problem looks like a nail." As we grow in our gifts, it's like we're adding tools to our toolbelt. The solutions we bring to the world—whether in business, art, finance, politics, family, or anything else—often have more to do with the tools we've acquired and mastered rather than what's actually possible.

When I first started out as an artist, I had very rudimentary skills. No matter how big the dream or how complex I wanted to go with my ideas, I only had a limited amount of skill, knowledge, understanding and wisdom from which to work. As I offered those to the Lord, He blessed and multiplied them. My faithfulness to enlarge my capacity by mastering my materials and techniques gave me many more creative options than I initially had. The same has been true in business. Because I've faithfully shown up to do my part in our co-laboring relationship, God uses my experience to speak to me about creative solutions. God gives the gifts and I am faithful to use and grow them. To the degree we are faithful in the process is the degree to which God will accelerate and multiply our efforts. That's how the Kingdom works.

## Satan Attacks our Uniqueness

It's easy to downplay your uniqueness in God's Kingdom when it seems everyone, including Satan, wants you to reject who God created you to be. And when your design and gift mix don't necessarily fit the mold of what's acceptable, it's easy to feel rejected. This is why knowing who you are in Christ is so important. In fact, in Ephesians 2:10, the Bible says that we are created as His masterpiece. That word 'masterpiece' comes from the word *poéma* which is where we get the word poem. Think of that! You are God's poem. The unique creative expression of God to reveal and release His nature into the world!

When we fail to intentionally embrace our unique design, gifts and graces, we forfeit God's plan for our life and often operate in comparison, shame, fear and manipulation—settling for the mundane life of a religious clone. We not only leave opportunities untapped, but also open the door for the enemy to use our areas of immaturity for his purposes.

## Wounds of the Heart

We all experience emotional, spiritual, or relational wounds in life. While God wants to use these difficulties to mature us, the enemy wants to use them to manipulate us in our areas of immaturity and get us to reject, deny or downplay our uniqueness.

Our wounds often leave us with feelings of inadequacy, jealousy, fear and a desire to manipulate people and circumstances in order to reduce or eliminate pain in our life. Inadequacy demands protection. Protection leads to performance pressure. Performance creates false personas designed to mask who we really are. Do that long enough and it's hard to tell the real you from the persona you've created out of a need to cope with a wound.

Unless we intentionally invite Jesus into the wounded places of our hearts and allow Him to heal us, we'll end up creating a real mess out of a desperate need to survive. Think of Lucifer as described in the book of Ezekiel 28—a beautifully created worship leader in the throne room of God. Covered in jewels, designed to reflect the beauty of God, he resonated with the sounds of God as the wind of the Spirit flowed through musical pipes embedded in his body. Talk about a design, wow! And yet, sin caused a separation. The very things God gave him to be a blessing laid the groundwork for his downfall as he operated in selfish pride and immaturity.

## Fear of Inadequacy

I have often wondered why people who achieve great success in their life—musicians, actors, performers, business people, inventors—experience stage fright, imposter syndrome and paralyzing fear. It doesn't make sense to the natural mind. They seem to have everything they want, yet it is a very real phenomenon that causes many of them to pull back altogether into what they perceive to be a safer place.

The temptation to quit, pull back and play smaller becomes stronger as we experience success. The stage is bigger. The stakes are higher. Feelings of inadequacy are magnified. Memories of past mistakes replay in our minds and areas of perceived vulnerability cloud our ability to see ahead and move forward. The only sure way to gain victory over this is to get rooted and grounded in the Love of God and in the identity He has established for us in His Word.

When you have a clear vision from the Lord regarding who you are and what you are called to in the Kingdom, you can walk in the assurance that His promises are greater than the current situation you may be facing. Protected and provided for by your Heavenly Father. Remember, this is God's story and you are a part of it. As you lean into His Love and grace, you will be able to walk strong.

## The Tension

Even with those who are strong in the Lord, there is always tension between the calling of God and their willingness to walk in it. Every great person of faith noted in the Bible experienced moments when the tension felt like it would kill them. Jesus in the Garden of Gethsemane the night before He was crucified. The prophet Jonah as he struggled to give the word God gave him for the city of Nineveh. Abraham, as he dealt with the competing emotions of obedience to God and his feelings of love for his son when God asked him to sacrifice Isaac. And yet, the choice to push through with tenacity and grace is the thing that made the difference.

Paul said it best, *"No, dear brothers and sisters, I have not achieved it, but I focus on this one thing: Forgetting the past and looking forward to what lies ahead, I press on to reach the end of the race and receive the heavenly prize for which God, through Christ Jesus, is calling us."* Philippians 3:13-14 NLT.

At some point, each one of us has to forget (as an intentional act of our will) all the stuff from our past—the inadequacies and mistakes, the vulnerabilities and the times we acted out of immaturity and fear—and step into the grace offered to us by the Father. Regardless of whether you feel like it or not, when you were saved you became a new creation in Christ. The tension asks you to make a choice—will you align with your new reality, or continue to live according to

*Without intentionality,*
*it is doubtful*
*any person will fully*
*recognize God's best*
*for their life.*

what makes sense to your old nature. Sometimes it happens in big decisions and other times, through small daily decisions. Big or small, it's your choice. It really is that simple.

## Intentional Pursuit of Maturity

Without intentionality, it is doubtful any person will fully recognize God's best for their life. Like Paul, you must choose to forget. You must stretch, lean and continue to walk. Cry out to God when times get tough but walk on. Know that God is faithful. He is your peace. He has not brought you this far to leave you. If you're in what feels like the valley of the shadow of death, He has prepared a place for you. A place of nourishment, strength and refreshment. In your weakness, His strength is made perfect. It's not all up to you because this is His story, empowered by His strength, for His purposes.

Awaken your heart and mind to the Holy Spirit's presence within you. Invite Him to do a deep work in you. Know He desires to restore your heart, dismantle the fear of inadequacy and destroy your need to protect and perform. He wants to reassure you of your identity in Christ, affirm your unique design and deepen your heart's connection to His. It's an ongoing process and a normal part of every believer's life. Here are a few principles to actively cultivate in your life that will enable you to embrace your unique design in a healthy way.

## Pursue Your Heart's Desire

Actively pursue the things that have always been in your heart. Don't give time, energy and attention to what others have said or even what you have believed was impossible. The more you encourage yourself in the Lord and step out in faith, the more confident you'll become in your ability to follow the Holy Spirit's leadership. As you cultivate your gifts, you'll see your capacity to flow with Him grow. And don't let the enemy place fear in your heart or convince you what God is calling you to do is somehow reckless. As you grow more confident in hearing God's voice in the context of your design and assignment, faith will grow. Walking in community with other believers and receiving their godly counsel will add another layer of confidence.

## Grow in Skill and Proficiency

Build skill and proficiency in the areas and attributes that make you unique. No matter what God calls you to do, I guarantee your unique design has a major part to play. God designed you uniquely for a reason, so celebrate it! The more you work to your strengths and build on what God has already deposited in you, the faster you'll see acceleration happen in your journey. You don't have to accel in everything. Only in the thing He designed you to do. That's why you are in the Body of Christ! As you walk with God, He will align you with others who have what you need and vice versa. Over time, God will use your uniqueness to set you apart. Especially if you're called to the marketplace. Let me give you an example.

When God called me back in 2009 to raise up an army of artists to reveal His Glory in the earth, I had a very ministry-centric view of what that would look like. It's the only tool I had in my toolbelt, or so I thought. But God showed me my full-time calling was both ministry and marketplace. At that time, I had very little understanding or a framework for living my full-time calling.

As I continued following the favor God poured into my life, I realized God was blessing my effort to encourage other artists from a spiritual perspective and, He was also blessing my business. I was creating unique work, meeting new clients, selling my work for thousands of dollars and developing quite a unique reputation as an artist in the marketplace. But something odd was happening. Every time I would speak to artists about the art and faith connection, they would ask me about the business side of things. They loved that God had created them to be an artist, but wondered how they could make a living from their art.

Marketing and the art business was something that came naturally to me. Partly because we had owned several small businesses over the years, partly because God wired me as a people person with an innate ability to connect and partly because He was teaching me how the Kingdom worked in the context of the marketplace. As I started putting the puzzle pieces of my own design, gifts and graces together, something unique emerged. As God gave me the experience, passion and vision to help artists connect with the God who created them to create, He showed me the pathway for them to thrive in the marketplace from a Kingdom perspective. A way to sell art without selling out. I could teach them how I learned to grow my business by learning to hear God's voice and recognize His leadership. That realization became the catalyst for our, Created to Thrive Artist Mentoring Program, which has helped thousands of artists around the globe step into everything God created them to be. As we continue to pursue all God has for us, the Thriving Christian Artist Podcast, books, live events and other opportunities we've sponsored over the years has created an abundant stream of income for me and my family. And the best part? God's unique expression set me apart from every other art marketing mentor in the world. That's the power of embracing your uniqueness and intentionally pursuing maturity in it.

## Learning to Hear God's Voice

Central to that maturing process is learning to hear God's voice. The more we develop confidence in our relationship with Him and our ability to recognize His voice, the quicker we'll respond to His leadership. As you take time with the Lord each day, pay attention to the seemingly random thoughts, feelings, images and words that come into your mind. Pay attention to the things that God highlights as you meditate on His Word and spend time in His presence. Write them down in a journal and ask the Lord to confirm what you're sensing. We'll talk more about this later, but trust me. As you cultivate the habit of actively listening for God's voice, you'll be amazed at what you begin to hear.

Fellow believers can also help us discern and confirm the things we feel are from the Lord as well as help us recognize areas of weakness and blind-spots. You have a unique part to bring, yet we also need the gifts, graces and design of others. That's Kingdom living.

As you do learn what it means to walk with God and others in your unique design, God will begin to enlarge your territory and expand your opportunities. Eternal fruit will begin to be produced in your life through the creative expression of His Kingdom inside you. And that's what the next chapter is all about: Expansion.

# Chapter 7

*Surprise, You're an Artist!*

There's no way I could have planned the life I'm walking in today. I'm still in awe and wonder at how God chose to move in and through my life as an artist and entrepreneur, speaker and worship leader. It's crazy and yet, it's my story. My God story. But here's the exciting news, my friend. You have a God story, too!

The story of your life has been written in God's book—an incredible story of provision and providence, light and life. And the most beautiful part? It's all God's idea! He's the one that designed you for the story. As you learn to co-labor with Him, you'll experience all He's created you for! That's the Kingdom.

One of God's first commands to humanity in Genesis 1:28 was to "be fruitful and multiply."

> *Expansion always comes*
> *as you are fruitful in what*
> *you've already been given.*

If you want to experience multiplication in the Kingdom, you must first be fruitful. A single piece of fruit has multiple seeds within it that can produce an exponential amount of additional fruit. Multiplication is the natural result. But first, the seed needs to be planted and nurtured.

## Creativity and the Kingdom

As we dive into this third concept of expansion in the IDEAL Framework, I want to let you in on a little secret. I'm not the only artist here. You are one too, whether you know it or not. When creating the world, God could have revealed Himself to humanity any way He desired. And yet, He chose to introduce Himself as a Creator, or as I want to suggest, an Artist. Our God is the only being who can create something out of nothing. He can also take disparate parts, seemingly unrelated and shape them into a thing of beauty that reveals His very nature. This is something He invites us to do in the Kingdom, too!

Consider Psalm 19:1-5 NLT when it says, "*The heavens proclaim the glory of God. The skies display His craftsmanship. Day after day they continue to speak; night after night they make Him known. They speak without a sound or word; their voice is never heard. Yet their message has gone throughout the earth, and their words to all the world.*"

The creative expression of God displays and proclaims His nature. It speaks a powerful message to everyone who has ears to hear. It carries His transforming power and changes people, atmospheres and nations when it is revealed. Wow! And yet here's the best part. As His children, we have the opportunity to co-labor with Him as

Kingdom artists—co-creating with Him so His transformative nature and Glory might be experienced by all. Just like the Father invited Adam into His creative process by letting him name the animals in the book of Genesis, He continues to invite us to participate with Him today. What an opportunity!

## Seeing Those Things that are Not

You might be thinking there's no way God made you an artist since you can't even draw a straight line with a ruler, but here's the truth—because you're Heavenly Father is an artist, you have His creative DNA inside of you. You have the ability to see those things that are not as though they were (Romans 4:17) and co-labor with the Holy Spirit to call them out and bring them forth into the earth realm. And whether that's a new business or invention, product or service, piece of art or a creative solution that can solve a world problem—it has the capacity to carry the light and life of God, transforming all those who interact with it.

*Creativity is not just for artists; it's how the Kingdom of God works for everyone. God's Kingdom expands as His power moves through the creative expression of His children in every area of society, bringing heaven to earth.*

Visual artists practice this faith principle of seeing those things that are not when we get an idea or an inspiring thought. It rolls around in our imagination until we have enough faith to make the awesome thing we envision. We then start to work creating that which previously existed only in our mind. In fact, every created thing started in the mind of a creator. Whether it's the chair you are sitting in or your favorite gadget. Before it became tangible, it was just an idea floating around in someone's mind. It's the creative process that brought it into being. The Kingdom of God works the same way.

As you connect with the heart of God, embrace your ideal design and pay attention to the ideas God brings your way, you'll have the opportunity to bring heaven to earth through your God-inspired creativity. Every child of God is meant to create with Him. It's the way the unique expressions of God's Nature and His Kingdom become incarnate on the earth. *God chooses to reveal Himself to the world through your life and the work of your hands.* That's incredible.

## The Process of Prophetic Creativity

As you consider your role in this creative Kingdom, I want to help you understand how the creative process works practically in the life of a believer. It looks like this: Relationship, Revelation, Agreement, Skillful Response, Incarnation, Transformation and Abundance.

When we enter into an intimate relationship with God, He begins to reveal things to us in a myriad of ways. As faith rises in your heart for the things He's showing you, give God your "yes" and respond skillfully with your gifts, talents and resources. Under the leading of the Holy Spirit, a nudge or idea becomes incarnate, real, tangible. A vehicle of transformation used by the Spirit of God. And, transformation leads to God's abundance being poured out. Someone may experience physical healing through an idea you birth into the world and through that, experience the abundant Love of God. Or someone's financial life could experience God's abundant provision because you were able to employ them. The opportunities are endless.

Don't overcomplicate this. Simply get with Jesus, do what He shows you and in faith, trust Him with the results. He will multiply and accelerate your efforts in ways you never thought possible. Why? Because this is how the Kingdom works. As you mature in the things He's called you to, God will expand your territory, increase your influence and grow your impact. And the more He does, the more opportunity you'll have to simply throw those things back at His feet as worship knowing that it's not about you and all about Him.

## Discovering Your Assignment

Now that you know God wants to use your creativity to release His transformative nature on the earth in order to reveal His Kingdom, it's vital you understand what God has called you to. He has an assignment for you. And your willingness to walk in your assignment in the context of your unique design is directly related to your ability to experience the abundant life Jesus promised.

One of the most common questions I get when mentoring people is, how do we know what God's plan is for our lives? They'd be glad to walk in it if they just knew what it was. Combine that with the fact that many church leaders encourage people to pursue God's plan without giving them the tools they need and we have a recipe for frustration and overwhelm which leads many people to simply give up. But that doesn't have to be your story. Today, that can change. But I want to give you a caveat: you can know God's plan for your life but it will always come with a bit of mystery and adventure attached. Don't worry, God's got your back. He is for you and is working on your behalf.

## Perfectionism

There is no surefire way you're going to know His perfect will for you 100% of the time or if what you are sensing is coming from Him. Thankfully, the Kingdom of God is not based in the fear that often drives our perfectionistic tendencies, but the invitation to experience God's grace day by day. God is more interested in a relationship with you that's built on trust and your willingness to operate by faith, rather than just dogmatic obedience. Remember, *"without faith, it's impossible to please God"* (Hebrews 11:6 NIV). Of course, God wants us to obey Him. We can't say we're followers of Jesus if we don't obey His commands. But that obedience must come out of a place of authentic relationship and faith-filled response, not just religious obligation.

Oftentimes, a strong desire to know God's exact plan has more to do with your perfectionistic comfort level than honoring God. Ouch! I know. That's a hard one, but it's true. We veil our real motives behind what seems like pure intentions. But really, we just want to know what to expect and how to respond. We want to be in the driver's seat. We want to self-protect by using performance and perfectionism as coping mechanisms for living rather than realizing they are often survival responses used to deal with past trauma. But God's Kingdom doesn't work like that.

*Trusting God always requires exchanging what you've known for what He's promised.*

He's looking for those willing to join Him in the adventure of Kingdom living even though it can feel like stepping into the unknown. The Father is inviting you into the glorious adventure in the Kingdom as you walk it out with Him over a lifelong journey. Don't worry. You can trust Him with your heart.

**God has a Plan for Your Life**

We know God has a plan for our lives because He told us in His Word here in 1 Corinthians 2:9-16 NLT, *"No eye has seen, no ear has heard, and no mind has imagined what **God has prepared** for those who love Him." But it was to us that **God revealed these things by His Spirit**. For His Spirit searches out everything and shows us God's deep secrets. No one can know a person's thoughts except that person's own spirit, and no one can know God's thoughts except God's own Spirit. And **we have received God's Spirit** (not the world's spirit), **so we can know** the wonderful things God has freely given us. When we tell you these things, we do not use words that come from human wisdom. Instead, we speak words given to us by the Spirit, using the Spirit's words to explain spiritual truths. But* *people who aren't spiritual can't receive these truths from God's Spirit. It all sounds foolish to them and they can't understand it, for* **only those who are spiritual can understand what the Spirit means.** *Those who are spiritual can evaluate all things, but they themselves cannot be evaluated by others. For, "Who can know the LORD's thoughts? Who knows enough to teach Him?" But we understand these things, for* **we have the mind of Christ.** *"*

In the passage of scripture above, I've taken the liberty of placing several sections in bold for emphasis. Clearly, Paul wants every believer to know God has prepared incredible, glorious things for us. And that He reveals them to us by His Holy Spirit and the supernatural mind of Christ. Wow! I hope that encourages you as much as it encourages me. We don't have to figure life out by ourselves, follow the crowd and do life like everyone else. There is a supernatural plan for our lives designed by God and we can know what it is and learn how to walk in it. And you can trust God will be walking with you every step of the way!

## How God Reveals His Plans

Understanding God's plan often begins with a passion, dream or vision. Sometimes it's through a literal dream or vision, a prophetic word from another person, or a revelation or impression that comes to us while in His presence. It can be as simple as recognizing the areas of favor and open doors in a certain area, or a desire that just won't go away. Regardless of the specifics, I've found it always culminates with a stirring in the heart for something more. A longing or desire to see the lives of others and/or the world enhanced or improved in some significant way. A passion to solve a big problem. Ultimately, that seed of inspiration will grow little by little until we can see it in our imagination, feel it in our hearts and have faith to start moving toward it.

It's easy to blame God when things don't come to fruition in our lives, but remember—God gives us the seeds of inspiration and we are responsible for nurturing them into fruitfulness. When a seed doesn't germinate, most of the time the problem is with the soil, not the seed. If you create the right environment for your seed with gratitude and expectancy, it will sprout and grow. But tempting as it may be, don't lose faith while your seed is still in the ground. At the right time, it will bring forth its intended fruit. You can count on it.

## Walk by Faith, Not by Sight

The Bible reminds us in 2 Corinthians 5:7 that we are to walk by faith, not by sight. In other words, we are to trust in what is unseen rather than what is seen. A philosophy that seems completely opposite to the way the world teaches us how to live. Instead of trusting what we can see, touch and measure physically — God asks us to fully trust what He says and what He's promised us.

Are you wondering how to bridge the gap between what you're experiencing now and what is promised? How can you confidently walk with God when you don't see His promises physically manifesting? Or, if it's possible to develop faith in something you've not yet seen in the natural? One primary way we can do all these things is through our redeemed imaginations.

The Holy Spirit lives inside every believer in Jesus. That's part of the salvation package. But unfortunately, most never ask Him for any guidance or revelation even though Holy Spirit's primary role is to be our comforter, teacher and guide. He remains the Christians greatest untapped resource. Willing, able and always available—yet seldom asked or acknowledged. You can change that.

As we invite the Holy Spirit to reveal God's plan for our life, our redeemed imagination will change what was only an abstract idea or vague hope into something we can see, feel, taste and interact with. How? Because once God shows you something, rest assured, it already exists in the realm of the Spirit. It's through our agreement with God's revealed plans and purposes that these things get released into our physical reality.

## Assembling the Puzzle

Of course, we would all love to receive a personal letter or text message detailing the intricate plans the Lord has for us in the next 25 years, but that's not how the Kingdom works. Probably because God knows that we would run ahead and try to accomplish everything on our own, in our own strength and for our own glory. At least that's been my tendency.

I've found discovering God's plan is more like finding and fitting the pieces of a puzzle together than having a golden scroll of revelation float down from heaven. That's the adventure. And that's why His plans must be based in both your identity in Christ and your unique design. Without this foundation, people often end up pursuing things that have nothing to do with their design or assignment. And when that happens, there's no peace, provision, opportunity, or favor. Why? Because all those things freely flow when we walk in alignment with how God created us.

God's plan is not something that He is going to force on you. It's something He's going to uncover with you as you involve the Holy Spirit in the process of discovery. Proverbs 16:9 NIV reminds us that, "*In his heart, a man plans his way, but the Lord orders his steps.*" In other words, when you start planning and pursuing the things God has placed on your heart, He will start ordering your steps. But it is your responsibility to initiate the planning process with Him. God plants the seed of inspiration and you respond in faith.

## God's Plan Evolves Over Time

It's important to remember that His plan for us evolves over time. It's not that He's playing games with us. Certainly not. I like to think of it as a plan that is ever unfolding based on the season of life I'm living in and how I've stewarded what He's entrusted to me thus far. It's like looking at a horizon line while you're walking. As long as you keep walking, the horizon line will keep changing. You may be walking in the same direction, but there are always new things ahead.

When God releases vision, it's often in the context of our current season or the one we are about to enter. Otherwise, if He were to show us everything at once, we would become overwhelmed and strive to make things happen in a way that makes sense to our natural mind. God gives vision to keep us inspired and heading toward the dream He has placed in our heart. But we can't let the vision we understand today become a barrier to the next thing God has for us tomorrow. Especially when it doesn't make sense in our natural mind. Demanding to know everything right now is not a beneficial way to live if we want to walk by faith. Walking with God by faith is a mysterious adventure as much as a journey inspired by vision. Either way—we can trust Him.

## Kingdom Convergence

One of the exciting dynamics of God's IDEAL plan is when God takes all the seemingly disparate parts of a person's life—all their experience, passion and skill—into a place of union for their fulfillment and His Kingdom purposes. I refer to this as convergence. The result is a dynamic and beautiful expression of God's Kingdom, unlike anything they've ever experienced.

It's incredible to watch a person realize that all the roads they've taken in their life, all the difficulties and refining moments they've walked through, have come together to flow as one river. A life they've only dreamed about—a supernatural process we could have never pre-planned. This is usually a real moment of breakthrough. Instead of continuing to search for the "thing" they're supposed to be doing for the Lord, they recognize He's been at work in and through "all things." They can envision what's possible in the context of what He's already formed and placed inside them, rather than how they don't yet measure up. It's much easier to receive vision for our life based on who God's already created us to be than who we think we need to be to serve Him.

**Without Vision**

Vision is central to how God leads us in His Kingdom. God releases vision for our lives through desire and design. He puts passion in our hearts for certain things, knowing that He's already created us with a design that can bring that passionate vision into reality. He stacks the deck in our favor because God wants us to thrive.

*Vision keeps us inspired when things are difficult and keeps us moving forward when we get overwhelmed by life.*

He offers vision as a measuring stick and standard by which we evaluate the opportunities that come our way—helping us focus on what is most important in our current season. Clear vision from God allows us to say yes to the right things and no to the wrong so we can invest our time, energy and resources in the most effective place in His ever-unfolding plan.

The Bible says in Proverbs 29:18 KJV, "*Where there is no vision, the people perish.*" That word vision isn't just the ability to see. It's actually prophetic revelation. And the word perish means to literally cast-off restraint. So, to rephrase it; "Where there is no prophetic revelation, the people cast off restraint." If we don't have a clear revelation from the Lord regarding who we are, how we have been designed and what He's calling us to, we'll run around full of

*When we are
faithful with what
God puts in our hand,
He will trust us
with more.*

frustration and having no focus. Not exactly God's IDEAL for our life.

## Faithful with Little

When we are faithful with what God puts in our hand, He will trust us with more. He expands the "field" we're working in and makes sure the resources we need are at our disposal. As we actively pursue our Kingdom assignment, God brings expansion and increase. Growth and acceleration are a natural part of the process when we respond with our "yes" and steward well what we've been given.

Remember the Parable of the Talents in Matthew 25? Jesus gave talents (up to 15 years of wages per talent, some say) to each of the 3 workers in the field based on their history. One guy received five talents, one guy two and another, one. In the story, the first two guys went and invested their money, doubling their investment. Upon returning, the master said to each in Matthew 23:23 NKJV, "*Well done, good and faithful servant; you have been faithful over a few things, I will make you ruler over many things. Enter into the joy of your lord.*"

This is a core principle in God's Kingdom: when you are faithful with little, God makes you ruler over much. When we walk fruitfully in the revelation, opportunities and resources we have, it demonstrates to God we can be entrusted with more. And there's no limit to what He will entrust to those whose hearts are completely His.

The guy with one talent went and hid his talent in the ground out of fear and his own feelings of inadequacy. Because he believed his master was a "hard man" and thought he couldn't measure up to his expectations, he took the safe route and hid everything so he wouldn't lose it. We often do the same when it comes to the investments God has given us. Instead of walking in confident faith and moving quickly toward what God has shown us to do, we shrink back in unbelief and hide our talents out of fear of loss.

Unfortunately for the guy in the story, that which he was given was taken from him and given to the others. The same is true for us. If we do not use the ideas, opportunities and resources God places in our hand, we run the risk of losing them. God will always bring other opportunities our way, but don't allow unbelief and feelings of inadequacy stop you from confidently pursuing what God has obviously placed in your path.

## Increase without Investment

Many people have five talent dreams, but one talent habits. They want all the benefits and blessings of multiplication but aren't willing to intentionally pursue their Kingdom assignment to see those things become a reality. They want increase without investment. They aren't willing to say no to things in their life that are distractions to their primary assignment. They refuse to draw consistent, healthy boundaries—on their time, focus, relationships and resources—resulting in constant feelings of overwhelm. Consequently, they become wimpy whiners, paralyzed poor-mouthers, or self-serving strivers. But to experience the blessing and favor of God in our lives, we must faithfully show up every day with what's in our hand, invite Him into our journey and follow His leading by faith.

Just like the boy who brought the five loaves and two fish to Jesus in the 'Feeding of the Five Thousand' in John 6, we must offer what we have to the Lord, even though it may not seem like much to us. Why? The Kingdom is a partnership. Jesus won't multiply the fish we never catch or the bread we never bake.

*Our faithfulness
activates God's willingness
to multiply our efforts.*

And when He does, just like in the story, there will be an overflow of leftovers for everyone to enjoy.

**Vision Create Boundaries**

People often ask me how I get so much work done and wonder if I ever sleep. Thankfully, God has multiplied my efforts over the years, but here's the truth. I have learned to be very selective about who and what I allow into my life. I know who God has created me to be and what He's called me to do in each season of life I'm in. Those are the things I readily say "yes" to. Understanding *God's IDEAL plan for my life has enabled me to create the boundaries in my life.* Everything else, no matter how good it may seem, usually gets a "no". That's not because I don't want to help others or I'm a selfish person. It means that I value my design and assignment and recognize the season I'm in. Aligning my priorities with my season has given me the confidence to be able to say "yes" to the right things and "no" to the wrong things in my life. It also gives me space in my schedule for enjoying life and time to respond to unavoidable emergencies that often arise.

## Hearing God's Voice, Following His Lead

Another primary way God leads us is through His voice. God is always speaking and every believer can hear His voice. That's part of the salvation package. Jesus said in John 10:27 ESV, "*My sheep hear my voice, and I know them, and they follow me.*" We were designed for intimate relationship with God and He speaks to us in a variety of ways including: His Word, the inner witness of the Holy Spirit, dreams, visions and even our redeemed imagination. He also brings people into our lives—mentors, leaders, parents, spouses, children and godly friends—to speak and encourage us to pursue His IDEAL plan. And of course, He uses the circumstances of life to get our attention and speak directly to our hearts.

The issue isn't whether God is speaking but whether we are taking the time to pay attention to how He's speaking. Taking time to slow down, ask, look, watch and listen is a required learned habit in Kingdom living. And when you recognize God speaking to you, it's important to receive it by faith, not dismiss it out of fear or unbelief just because it doesn't make sense to your natural mind. Remember, in James 1:6-8 NJKV it says, "*But let him ask in faith, with no doubting, for he who doubts is like a wave of the sea driven and tossed by the wind. ⁷ For let not that man suppose that he will receive anything from the Lord; ⁸ he is a double-minded man, unstable in all his ways.*"

Being double-minded is one of the greatest enemies to faith because it causes us to turn our eyes away from what God has promised and onto the physical reality around us. Our minds and hearts begin to wonder if what God said and promised is really true. When God speaks to your heart, receive it as a treasure and protect it with singular focus.

## Lord, is that Really You?

Sometimes people worry whether what they are hearing internally is from the Lord or not. That's a valid concern but not an excuse to walk in fear. Here's why. You can always measure what you think God is saying by what you know about His Word and His nature. His spoken words, visions, impressions, or revelations will never contradict what's written in the Bible. The better we know His Word and His nature, the more confident we'll be in recognizing and responding to His voice. And don't worry. If you miss it, there's grace. Sometimes you'll get it right and other times you won't. Neither change His Love or commitment to you. He promises to never leave our side.

One of the most exciting and endearing things I've discovered about the Lord is this:

*God speaks most clearly in the context of our unique design and assignment.*

We honor His presence best as we honor our design. Once we align with who He says we are and what He says we can do, hearing God's voice becomes a lot easier. Artists often hear God best when they are creating. Business people often hear best when they are building and strategizing. Teachers often hear best when they are researching and sharing their new revelation with others. We hear God best in the language He designed us to hear Him through. Do you long to hear God more clearly and consistently? Do what He created you to do. It's like paving a superhighway of connection right to the heart of God.

No matter how God speaks to you, it's important to write down what He says. And over the years, I've found journaling is a great way to do that. It's one of the most productive and life-giving habits I've ever employed. Through the daily habit of writing down my prayers, celebrating my successes, expressing my disappointments, declaring my thankfulness and then taking time to listen to God's responses—I am continually filled. Filled with His presence and comfort, with His Love for me and all He's called me to. And filled with encouragement and ideas for the day, knowing He's walking with me every step of the way. I even revisit my journals from years gone by every now and then, just to celebrate how far God has brought me on my journey. If you're not someone who journals, I'd encourage you to start. There's no right or wrong way to do it and you can't mess it up. So, just start and do it in a way that works for you.

I remember this one time. I was journaling with the Lord and saw myself in the spirit walking with Jesus. His arm was around my shoulder like a comforting friend. As we walked, I noticed angels going before us. They were clearing the path of rocks and things that could cause me to trip and fall. A beautiful, visual example of Psalm 91:11-12 NLT, where it says *"For He will order His angels to protect you wherever you go. They will hold you up with their hands so you won't even hurt your foot on a stone."* Seeing myself with Jesus in that moment, through the eyes of my redeemed imagination, strengthened my faith. It encouraged me to take hold of the promise and gave me supernatural confidence to continue. At that moment, the Holy Spirit taught me an important lesson.

> *Faith in God's promises*
> *activates God's power*
> *within us.*

## Perception vs Penalty

One of the principles I try to employ in my own journaling practice is to allow my times with the Lord to be more about perception than penalty. To become aware of what God is saying. To become conscious of what He is showing me, rather than focusing on whether I'm getting everything exactly right and the consequences of getting it wrong. As I discern a thought, feeling or image is from the Lord—I trust God's heart and the leadership of the Holy Spirit in the mystery.

The word perceive is defined as becoming aware or conscious of something. It's like awakening to a reality that's been there all long.

*Learning to hear
God's voice
always requires a
step of faith.*

I encourage you to cultivate your awareness of what the Holy Spirit is saying and showing you through every sense and resource God has given you. Learning to hear God's voice is about prioritizing our ability to perceive rather than the pressure of getting perfect results.

When we connect a penalty to a thought we think is coming from us and not from God, because it doesn't make sense to our natural mind, we block the new innovative thing God is trying to show us. Remember, God often speaks in ways that are hard to understand with our natural mind. He may give you a seed of inspiration, a secret strategy, or simple instructions that don't seem like they could lead anywhere. But if our immediate response is "no", we act out of fear rather than faith and we become double-minded.

Learning to hear God's voice always requires a step of faith. As you learn to trust the Holy Spirit to lead and guide you, you will become more confident in taking faith steps toward what God is showing you. Instead of attaching a penalty to the things that don't make sense, I encourage you to simply thank the Lord and write them down without the fear of getting it wrong. Then, in conversations with trusted friends and leaders in your life, you can determine which things are from the Lord and which are not. Which things you need more revelation on or what things are for now and what things may be for later. Sometimes, those far off glimpses are the most fun because even when we don't fully get it yet, we can trust the Lord to confirm His Word as we walk it out with Him.

No one gets it right 100% of the time. But remember, you're not performing for God. You're walking with God as His child and learning how to cultivate your Spirit-led perception with the Holy

Spirit as your guide. Some things you'll get and some things you'll miss. It's ok. He loves you. You'll learn and be sharper next time. Don't allow perfectionism and fear of penalty rob you of the joy in your journey.

## Impact & Influence

As you faithfully pursue your Kingdom assignment in the context of your unique identity and design—impact and influence are the natural result. Rarely does it happen the way we expect or in our timeframe, but it always happens. Just like we see throughout the Bible, God is looking to place faithful men and women in positions of influence to expand His Kingdom on the earth.

Consider Joseph. Born into obscurity but with the raw gifts of leadership, discernment and the ability to speak. But these alone were not enough. They had to be tested and matured for God to really use Him in a place of significant influence. He was rejected by his brothers, sold into slavery and tempted in every way. Through the trials of relationship, finances, seduction, power and revenge, he was found faithful. And because he was faithful, God promoted Him into a place of influence, impact and fulfillment in his generation.

Remember Esther? The Bible says that she was both beautiful and obedient. Two qualities specifically needed in the person God wanted to use to influence a King. And knowing how God used her, I think it's safe to say she was extremely courageous and smart, too. She knew what to say, when to speak and when to stay quiet. And guess what? God saw Ether's faithfulness and decided to use her for His purposes. Through difficulty and turmoil, she was faithful. God placed Esther in the Kings palace for impact and influence—for such a time as this.

And what about Moses? Plucked from the river and positioned by God from the very beginning of His life, he became a prince of Egypt. But that didn't mean he was free from tests and trial. He had to endure much difficulty in his maturing process, including being banished for killing an Egyptian. He was 80 years old before God called him to lead his people out of bondage. Even then, he had the privilege to lead a grumbling and complaining people. His faithfulness in the process of refinement was used by God to set a nation free.

What would have happened if Joseph got offended at his brothers and went off course? What if Esther had decided to talk more than God told her to when she went before the King? What would have happened if Moses had lost his temper with the Pharoah instead of doing what God said, the way God said to do it? Although it may not seem like it, you and I are being positioned in our generation—just like Joseph, Esther and Moses were in theirs. Positioned to set the captives free. Positioned to reveal and release His transforming power in the world. Positioned to declare the goodness of God that shifts atmospheres, cities and nations. But we must be willing to endure the maturing process.

## He's Looking for Your Yes

God's not looking for our perfection. He's looking for our "yes"! We don't have to measure up to an unattainable standard of perfection for Him to use us. HE can use us at any time in our journey. As we give God our "yes" on a daily basis, He will lead and equip us to walk in our ideal assignment. Cultivating an active pursuit of God's presence means we must be willing to get in His presence, adopt a new identity in Christ, embrace our unique design and actively pursue our Kingdom assignment. We can't live in the Kingdom on autopilot. Even though it's not all up to us, it is our responsibility to faithfully show up. As we do, expansion is the natural result.

*As God expands
our opportunities and influence,
He aligns us
for maximum fruitfulness.*

# Chapter 8

*Alignment for Your Assignment*

During my early years as a full-time, professional working artist (and by default, an entrepreneur), God started teaching me in a more accelerated way about faith and how the Kingdom worked. I had to reorient my thinking from striving on my own to cooperating with Him. God showed me that *being self-employed did not mean I was self-sufficient.* On the contrary, as I leaned in to the Lord and responded to His leadership, my walk of faith became richer. It was then I started seeing results. My business grew and my personal fulfillment increased. God began to use me in ways I never expected or thought possible. But like everyone, I was on a journey of maturity.

I remember going to an art show in Baltimore one February, believing in total faith God was going to do incredible things that weekend. This show was a big deal in my world. I was not only believing for divine appointments but also for great sales. In my mind there was a lot riding on the show regarding the success of my art business. God had the same goal in mind, but a different way of achieving it in my life.

When the show ended that Sunday night, I was more than disappointed. I barely made enough in sales to cover my expenses and I still had an eight-hour drive back to Asheville ahead of me the next day. I was not in a good place. On the ride home, I started having what we call in the south a "Come to Jesus" meeting. And I let Him have it. After I fully expressed my anger and disappointment at God for why this faith thing wasn't working for me, even though I did everything I thought I was supposed to do, He started talking.

Over the next eight hours, the Lord showed me where I had come out of alignment with His plan for my business. Early on in my business God had told me He would bring clients to my studio so I could live and create from a place of rest without the stress and cost of traveling to sell my art. I would only have to travel for ministry engagements. But I didn't listen. I started building my business like every other artist—traveling around the region and country doing shows. They were profitable, but they took a lot out of me.

As I drove home that day, I realized this was a refining moment for me. I had a choice. To listen to His voice and respond quickly or keep doing what I was doing. I chose to listen and respond in faith. After repenting for my disobedience, I asked the Lord what to do. I thought I heard Him say I was to go back and get the studio ready to sell. What? I didn't want to sell the studio! But as we continued to talk, I realized He wanted me to significantly redesign my studio space to create an environment more conducive to selling my work. Until then, my studio was a bohemian paradise of rough working space and thrift store furniture. And I wasn't selling very much at all from there.

Once home, I told my wife what I felt the Lord wanted me to do at the studio and she agreed. We invested in the changes He led us to make—lighting, display space, signage, etc.—and thankfully, it only took about 2 weeks. The first Saturday I opened after the renovations were finished; a couple walked in. After making small talk, they told me they planned to come see my work at the show in Baltimore but had not been able to attend. So, they decided to travel to Asheville to meet me and commission a piece. I was stunned. That day, they commissioned me to make a single basket for the cost of $2,000, my most expensive piece to date. As they walked out, I could almost hear the Lord laughing—for that's how His Kingdom is supposed to work. That was the beginning of my doing business by divine appointment.

## Getting into Position

Alignment, which is the fourth part of the IDEAL Framework, simply means getting into position. It's a series of micro-decisions we make, moment by moment and day after day, that get us more in tune with God so we can fully embrace our identity, design and assignment. Over time, these small decisions turn into habits that establish us and produce the fruit of the Kingdom.

As we intentionally plant His Word in our hearts—instead of living according to our feelings, perspective, or the opinion of others— everything changes. The little seed of inspiration you once gave a faint "yes" to will become a powerful movie inside your heart that you can see, touch and feel. And the lens through which you see everything will also change. You will no longer believe the lies of the enemy, but instead believe God. You'll embrace your unique design and pursue your Kingdom assignment instead of competing with others and chasing after greener pastures.

## Get in the Flow

One day the Lord showed me a simple analogy that's become a great reminder for me when it comes to understanding alignment. Imagine you've been working in your garden all day and you want to get a shower before dinner. You imagine how refreshing it will be as you turn on the faucet. Much to your surprise, the water is flowing out of the showerhead but you're not getting wet. You get frustrated and start to become upset. After working all day, now you can't even get a shower. So, you run to the home supply store and get a new shower head. You install it, turn the water on and nothing. You call the plumber and they come to the house for a service call. After an hour, they confirm everything is working correctly. But you're still not getting wet. Then, in a moment of illumination, you realize that although you've been standing in the shower, you weren't standing under the showerhead. The water was flowing freely the whole time but you weren't standing in its path.

The same is true in the Kingdom. God promises to bless us, provide for us, lead and protect us. This is a truth we can always count on. He is always setting up divine appointments, releasing new ideas and opening doors for us. But if we do not intentionally embrace and pursue our unique design and assignment in the Kingdom, we can't recognize or take advantage of the things God is bringing our way. You may have the best intentions in the world and love Jesus with your whole heart, but if you're standing outside the flow of God's provision, you're not going to receive all He has for you.

## Refinement for Your Assignment

God is always working to align and refine us so we can receive every good thing He has for us. But, He also allows us to walk through challenging situations or seasons that will mature and refine us. And most of the time, they are not seasons or situations we would choose for ourselves. Relational difficulties, frustrating situations at work, or financial blowouts are not God's best for us and the enemy uses them to turn up the heat in our life with the purpose of taking us out. But, thankfully, *"...we know that God causes everything to work together for the good of those who love God and are called according to His purpose for them."* Romans 8:28 NLT. You weren't designed to live alone in the valley of the shadow of death, but walk through it with God.

Just like you, I can think of situations I've been through that I never want to repeat. Yet, God used them to refine me for His purposes. Walking through seasons of refinement with the Lord enlarges our capacity to receive everything He has for us. For example, during the housing crash of the mid/late 2000's, we lost our marketing business, experienced some major betrayal and almost lost everything we had. That was on top of the hardship of leaving a successful ministry position in 2003 amid a church split. It was a horribly difficult time for us. And unfortunately, we didn't know how the Kingdom worked at the time, especially regarding our finances.

Consequently, I went into panic mode and flailed around, bouncing from job to job, searching for anyway I could make money and survive. After several years of bouncing, I found myself laid off from my latest job and feeling desperate. I had no other options left—so

I cried out to God while sitting in the parking lot of a local business. I asked Him what to do and He told me to go, home, lay on the floor and worship Him and that His provision would come like popcorn. Although I didn't fully understand what that meant, I did it. And it opened the greatest season of fulfillment and fruitfulness in my life to that point.

## Raise Up an Army

It was during that season of focused prayer and worship that the Lord woke me up two mornings in a row at 3:09 am with a song running through my mind about raising up an army like the one in the book of Joel. I went down to my studio and opened Joel 3:9 and read the passage which described raising up an army. I asked the Lord what it meant and He told me He was calling me to be a father to artists. I was to go to the nations and raise up an army of artists to reveal His Glory in the earth. In the middle of what felt like my lowest point, God spoke life to my identity, design and Kingdom assignment. When I finally surrendered my striving, He brought unimaginable breakthrough and alignment.

What happened next was incredible. As I gave God my "yes", He started opening doors for me in ways I could have never imagined. Immediately, financially profitable work started coming where many of my gifts converged. God spoke to me about visiting an art gallery and the woman running the place literally gave it to me two weeks later to house our new ministry to artists. Artists gathered there weekly, talking about the Kingdom and selling artwork. Their lives started to be transformed. It was an amazing time.

I will share more in just a moment but here's the main point I want you to understand. God used those very difficult moments in my life to refine and prepare me for what was next. Not because He was trying to destroy me, but because He wanted to bring me into everything He had for me in the Kingdom. There's no way I could have stepped into all I'm walking in now unless I allowed Him to deal with some deep issues in my life.

## Spinning Your Wheels

When we refuse to allow God to refine us, it's like pressing the brake and the gas in our car at the same time. It looks and feels like we're doing all the right things. There's a whole lot of smoke, but unfortunately, we're just spinning our wheels. That's a frustrating place to be. But it's not always as simple as it seems on the surface. We say we want to experience the blessing and benefits of the Kingdom, yet we're not willing to let go of the unhealthy ways we've been living. The pain and discomfort seem too great. I'm not only talking about sin here. Of course, we need to let those go. But many times, refining is about exchanging good for better and better for best.

*Growth in the Kingdom is always based on an invitation to more, not an accusation of not being enough.*

God invites us to face our giants, step into our promised land and pursue our God-given dreams. Why? Because He loves us. When we live below the promises of God, He will always invite us into more. In those moments, we can choose God's best or continue to walk in frustration. Take your foot off the brake!

## Opportunity to Respond

Every time God gives you a promise or shows you a vision of what could be, it comes with an opportunity to respond. Whether that promise is from His Word, something He's spoken to you or a dream He's placed on your heart. God's freedom is always on the other side of fear, if you face it by faith. Why? Because

## *Faith sets God's promises in motion.*

I love the declarative promise in Isaiah 54:1 NIV where it says, *"Sing, barren woman, you who never bore a child; burst into song, shout for joy, you who were never in labor; because more are the children of the desolate woman than of her who has a husband, says the LORD."* God is declaring His purposes over His people. But it wasn't a done deal with no responsibility on their part. No! Look what it says immediately after this in verses 2 – 5, *"Enlarge the place of your tent, stretch your tent curtains wide, do not hold back; lengthen your cords, strengthen your stakes. For you will spread out to the right and to the left; your descendants will dispossess nations and settle in their desolate cities. Do not be afraid; you will not be put to shame. Do not fear disgrace; you will not be humiliated. You will forget the shame of your youth and remember no more the reproach of your widowhood. For your Maker is your husband— the LORD Almighty is His name— the Holy One of Israel is your Redeemer; He is called the God of all the earth."*

See the pattern? Promise in verse 1, then opportunity to respond and make room for the promise in verse 2. Verses 3-5 are encouragement about their identity, who God is and what they need to do to step into the fullness of the promise.

## *Every promise from God comes with an opportunity to respond.*

Our ability to respond in faith requires us to renew our mind according to His truth. That's how God's Kingdom works.

### Resisting Refinement

When we resist or refuse our refining moments, we end up performing and striving in our own strength. We create "Ishmaels" that distract us and ultimately waste valuable time, energy and resources on things God never intended us to. We go around and around the same proverbial mountain until we finally submit to the refinement or run away. But when we trust God to bring us into maturity and cooperate with the growth process, we can experience acceleration and momentum in our life. Promotion and increase come from the Lord. It's all a matter of perspective.

## Lift Your Vision Higher

Alignment in the Kingdom always requires a change in our perspective. It invites us to lift our vision higher. Instead of focusing our attention on the things that so easily entangle, frustrate and make us angry—we need to ask Jesus if our situation is related to our personal refinement. What is His purpose in the situation, season, or relationship? When we only view our circumstances through our natural mind, we miss the transformational moments offered to us by God.

I've found that God often takes us through refining moments immediately preceding a moment of promotion. We can see, feel and taste the growth that's coming but know it's going to require something of us before we can enter our promised land. Before the Israelites could inhabit the land God had promised them, they had to face and defeat their giants. The same is true with us. We can either face our giants as they emerge and conquer them through the power of the Holy Spirit or avoid them out of fear and stay stuck in frustration. The choice is up to us.

## Facing One of My Giants

Years ago, I came face to face with one of my biggest giants. I had an overwhelming, visceral fear of exposure. Not physically, but internally. Let me explain. As a result of traumatic experiences, I had been through in my life, I felt as if the person who I was on the inside was bad, flawed and shameful. Subconsciously, I felt it necessary to protect myself from anything that would expose who I really was. It became a full-time job. I worked very hard to create a persona of perfection where everything looked good all the time. Bright and shiny with no chinks in the armor.

But underneath was a deep-seated fear that I would make a mistake and everything would come crashing down. My business, my finances, my reputation and my family—all gone in the blink of an eye, or so it seemed in the movie that was playing inside my mind. It was so real that anytime a situation would seem threatening, it would trigger strong reactions in me—all the way from physical pain and nausea to full-on panic attacks.

Unfortunately, after many years of unsuccessfully dealing with this issue, it kept coming back around. Every time, a little worse. Fears and mirages of destruction. Sidelined and psyched out. Satan was trying to use it to take me out. God allowed me to go through the pain to show me that area of my heart that needed to be healed. I won't go into all the gory details, but I finally hit an episode too big to ignore. It hit me like a ton of bricks.

One of my friends told me that until I dealt with the giant holding me hostage, I wouldn't be able to walk any further into my promised land. In this difficult moment, through the help of my wife and godly mentors, I was able to gain God's perspective. I was reminded that God wasn't trying to destroy me, but to make me into His image and bring me into greater fruitfulness. The Father disciplines those He loves (Hebrews 12:3-11) and prunes those branches that are already producing fruit (John 15:2). His faithfulness to lead me through this difficult season of refinement was for my good. After

*Fear often reveals areas of our heart where we don't yet fully trust the Lord.*

many tears, vulnerable conversations with trusted friends and some intense times of healing with the Lord, I faced my giant. I allowed God into that deep part of my heart that had been hidden for so long. And He healed me.

Fear often reveals areas of our heart where we don't yet fully trust the Lord. When fear arises, choose to see it as an invitation to wholeness and freedom rather than a threat to your existence. Now when I face similar types of triggering thoughts or situations, I try to see them from a healed and whole perspective. As I do, I'm able to walk through them empowered by the healing presence of Jesus, rather than the dominating fears of the enemy. The same is possible for you.

## Alignment for Your Assignment

As we stay close to Him through our refining process, God will purposefully align us in our specific Kingdom assignment. He will bring the ideas, opportunities, resources and relationships we need into our lives at the exact moment we need them. And He uses the knowledge, understanding and wisdom we've gained from our refining experiences to give us increased authority for our next season.

God also promises to bring abundant provision into our lives so we can accomplish the assignment He's given us. Yet, so many Christians struggle with the concept of God as abundant provider because they've been taught a false gospel that celebrates poverty and lack rather than God's abundant provision. So let me make this important distinction: you can walk in the abundant blessings and benefits of God's Kingdom as long as the blessings and benefits don't own your heart.

The Bible is often mistakenly quoted as saying, money is the root of all evil. That's a bold-faced religious lie that seeks to keep God's children from walking in the fullness of God's abundant and generous provision! Paul clearly states in 1 Timothy 6:10 that it's the <u>love of money</u> that is the root of all kinds of evil. Primarily because it causes people to lust and walk away from their faith. In fact, anything that replaces the primacy of Jesus in your life is an idol, a root where evil will sprout in your life. Money is simply a tool that we can use for the glory of God as we walk in our unique design and Kingdom assignment.

*God can trust those whose hearts are completely His with abundant resources to do all He's called us to do.*

He will gladly fulfill the desires of your heart and enable you to be a huge blessing to others at the same time. Remember, God's Word declares in Psalm 37:4 ESV, "*Delight yourself in the Lord, and He will give you the desires of your heart.*" David wrote it under the inspiration of the Holy Spirit but he also knew it to be true in his own life. You can too!

## Struggling with Lack

If you love Jesus and are pursuing Him with your whole heart but still struggle with a lack of money, resources, or opportunities in this season of your life, it's not because He doesn't love you or desire to provide for your every need. God's promises are yes and amen to those who love Him. More than likely, you're dealing with one or more common issues.

You might struggle to believe God will provide for you because of your life experience, the opinion of others or a lack of knowledge regarding His promises. And that leaves you believing you have to make it all happen on your own rather than receiving your provision by faith.

You could also be struggling because you're pursuing opportunities in areas that aren't God's plan for you. Maybe God designed you to be an entrepreneur and you're working a dead-end job for someone else. Or maybe He designed you to be an artist, yet you took the safe route and became an accountant. You pursued income opportunities that made sense in your natural mind, but since they don't align with your design and assignment, there's no real fruit. Even worse, it's caused you to strive and because you're trying to make things happen in your own strength, you either burn out or walk way below what God intended for you.

Maybe it's the back and forth of double-mindedness. One day you believe and then the next day you don't, all because of your circumstances. This shuts down your faith and causes you to respond to life in fear. Consequently, you don't pursue new opportunities and you don't steward well the things God has already entrusted to you. You're living life on pause.

If you're thinking, "Matt, I've done all of this and more", don't worry. You're in good company. I was a double-minded striving doubter. But thankfully, just like me, you're learning what God's Kingdom is all about and how to align your life with His Word. Once you do, things will absolutely change for you like they did for me.

For much of my life, I couldn't figure out why other people walked in such favor and blessing while I continued to struggle. I would try to make something happen and experience a little success but without the grace to maintain it long term. Conversely, I also experienced the frustration of working jobs that didn't pay me enough to support my family and pursue my dreams. Neither were God's best for my life.

I now realize, God didn't love them more, as the enemy tried to convince me many times. It was simply because I hadn't learned how to come into alignment with who God created me to be. Once I did, double doors of favor opened in my life creatively, personally, relationally and financially. Not because God somehow got in a good mood, but because I came into agreement with who He created me to be and His unique plans for my life. As I did, He positioned me for an amazing number of divine appointments.

## Divine Appointments

My life has been a series of supernatural divine appointments where God placed me at the right place, at the right time, to meet the right people—all so I could take advantage of the right opportunity. As I look back, none of it could have been orchestrated by me. Like many things with the Lord, they came suddenly and out of the blue. Because I kept saying "yes" to the refining hand of God and "yes" to the assignment He had for me, the doors kept on opening. Let me give you a few examples.

During my early years in ministry in the late 1990's, I was working as a youth pastor / worship leader in a denominational church plant. It was headed in what we now term a "seeker sensitive" direction. I enjoyed it because, in my experience, it felt new and fresh. But there was so much more. One day a fellow youth pastor in the area gave me a compliment, telling me I sounded just like the worship leader from the Brownsville Revival down in Pensacola, Florida. I thought, revival? That's cool. We had a spring and a fall revival, but not an ongoing revival. What could that be about? He handed me a Charisma magazine, which I had never seen before and on the back was an advertisement for a worship conference Brownsville was hosting. I had no idea what I was signing up for, but I knew I was supposed to go.

Once there, I spent three days on the floor worshipping Jesus. The presence of God was so strong in those meetings, I could hardly stand. I had never heard people singing in the Spirit and worshipping God like this before the preaching. The Glory of the Lord moved like waves through that place. Healing, deliverance and salvations were happening all around me. I was forever changed as I worshiped in His presence like never before. I was no longer satisfied with church as usual.

## Fired

When I came back to my home church, I was no longer on the same page. I wanted others to experience the depths of worship I had experienced, not just the abbreviated worship that had become the warmup for the sermon. Yes, I was immature at the time and, no, I didn't know how to walk that out in a good way. Looking back, I would have handled it all much differently. Consequently, a year later I was given the left foot of fellowship and shown the door.

That response devastated me. Newly married, we had just sold our first home to move closer to this church and were living in the guest bedroom of one of my worship team members at the time. Even though it felt like the rug had been pulled out from under us, I knew God had more. Through a series of divine appointments, God provided a 3-month interim job for me at a charismatic Episcopal church (I didn't even know that was a thing) that not only paid the bills, but taught us more about the supernatural and prophetic, positioning me for my next step in ministry.

## The Suddenlies of God

Knowing that interim opportunity was coming to an end, a friend who knew my heart for revival and worship said I should meet a leader who had recently planted a church not far from us. He was associated in some way with the Brownsville Revival School of Ministry so I reached out. Their leaders invited me to come to a service that Sunday night where Pastor John Kilpatrick from Brownsville would be preaching. Worship was electric that evening and he preached on the "suddenlies" of God. At the end, I went up for prayer and again—boom! Back on the floor, weeping under the power of God.

Afterwards, I met the pastor of that local church and he invited me to attend a service the next morning for leaders in the area. I showed up and for some reason, there was no worship leader. Come to find out, they had been flying a worship leader in from Pensacola every weekend to lead worship at the new church in North West Metro Atlanta. Since he wasn't able to be there that morning, they were just going to play pre-recorded music for worship. But instead, the pastor asked me if I wanted to lead that morning. I was shocked but I agreed. As I started leading worship, God's presence filled the room in a beautiful way. Over the next few weeks, I continued to develop a relationship with the leadership team of that church. Finally, we came to believe God had brought me there to become their worship leader. But we wanted confirmation.

That next Sunday, a prophet came to speak at the church and I was co-leading worship. No one told him they were considering me for a position. But as soon as worship ended, the man asked where the guy who was playing the piano, was. My wife and I stood up and he began to prophesy over us. He essentially told our whole life story up until that point and confirmed that God had brought me there to be the worship leader. In a moment, I was supernaturally set in place for one of the most pivotal and fruitful seasons of my life.

## Right Place, Right Time

There's no way I could have imagined any of that, much less planned it. But through a series of situations that often seemed like a dead end, God lead me through both the refining and defining process to position me at the right place at the right time with the right people. The only thing I did was recognize the opportunities by His grace and say "yes" along the way. As I've continued to grow in the Lord, that's still my standard operating procedure.

When I considered writing my first book in 2009, *Unlocking the Heart of the Artist*, I knew nothing about writing a book. But God just happened to place an experienced writer and editor in my circle of friends who helped me through the process. And when I had no clue how to get it out in the marketplace, God connected me with a man who became a significant spiritual father in my life, Ray Hughes. By writing the forward to that book, he gave it instant credibility and allowed me to stand on his shoulders in ministry. That kind of favor doesn't normally happen and I'm forever grateful.

When we moved to Asheville, North Carolina in 2009 (another supernatural suddenly), I was making my baskets as a serious hobby. But God had promised to use them in my calling of "ministry and marketplace". At the time, I was selling my baskets for $25-$50 each. Within 3 years of me moving to Asheville, I had been inducted into one of the nation's most prestigious fine craft guilds, started selling my work for hundreds and then thousands of dollars and was even included on a registry created by the Smithsonian American Art Museum's Renwick Gallery for American Artists Under 40. I was introduced to people I should never have been able to meet, giving me access to resources I should never have had access to. I won an award at an international art competition in Europe. I was featured in magazines. God connected me with many high-net-worth clients who began purchasing and commissioning my work as well as referring me to their friends. Pretty soon, my business started producing six figures and then, multiple six figures per year. That kind of growth and acceleration just doesn't happen in just a few short years. But God.

In 2012, I received a prophetic word in Scotland that God was going to amplify my voice through media. I had no clue what it meant, but I said "yes". I experimented with a few things and even did a live radio show in our town for a short season. Nothing seemed to work. Then, the Lord took me through a difficult season of refinement. When I came out on the other side, things really started to accelerate. God gave me a clear vision for equipping artists through an online mentoring program. He even brought someone to teach me exactly how to do it through a course that required an investment of $1500. I was nervous, but I did it and finished in record time. God then brought the team I needed to create my own artist mentoring program. Now years later, I've helped thousands of artists all over the world step into their Kingdom assignment and thrive spiritually, artistically and in business through our mentoring program, books, podcasts and events. He's taught me how to create an extremely effective and profitable business that not only helps people but gives me the financial provision I need for every ministry He's placed on my heart. Every step along the way, He's brought the right people and the right resources at the right time for whatever I needed. There has never been a moment of lack. Ever.

## Everything is Possible

I could write many books about the stories of how God has supernaturally led me throughout my life. But this isn't about me. It's about you. God is no respecter of persons. If He's done these

*Abundant provision
in the Kingdom
is a promise based on
our position,
not our performance.*

kinds of things and greater in my life, He will do the same and even greater in yours. The only caveat is; you need to be aligned with Him. Remember, God's not looking for your perfection. He's looking for your "yes". And when you give God your "yes", the refining process will begin. As you stay close to Him and pursue the vision He's given you under the leading of the Holy Spirit, He will intersect your path with everything you need in abundance. Faithfully show up. Every day, stay in faith and keep walking toward the vision He's given you.

Remember, abundant provision in the Kingdom is a promise based on our position, not our performance. You don't have to earn it. You're His child. You simply receive it by faith as you align with Him and the purpose's He's called you to in the Kingdom. Everything is possible.

As you walk with the Lord, He will bring provision to you in many different ways. Some that make sense to your natural mind and others that don't. Regardless of how He chooses to provide, it's important to remember that your heart should be connected to God as your provider, not the things He's provided for you or the ways He's provided for you.

*Even when God changes the way He provides, it does not change His promise to provide.*

## A New Way of Thinking

One of the most beautiful passages in all of scripture where Jesus describes this new dynamic is in Matthew 6:25-34 NLT. Here, Jesus helps the disciples to reorient their thinking to a new Kingdom perspective about provision—not only spiritual blessings, but their practical physical needs as well. He says, *"That is why I tell you not to worry about everyday life—whether you have enough food and drink, or enough clothes to wear. Isn't life more than food, and your body more than clothing? 26 Look at the birds. They don't plant or harvest or store food in barns, for your heavenly Father feeds them. And aren't you far more valuable to Him than they are? 27 Can all your worries add a single moment to your life?" 28 "And why worry about your clothing? Look at the lilies of the field and how they grow. They don't work or make their clothing, 29 yet Solomon in all his glory was not dressed as beautifully as they are. 30 And if God cares so wonderfully for wildflowers that are here today and thrown into the fire tomorrow, He will certainly care for you. Why do you have so little faith?" 31 "So don't worry about these things, saying, 'What will we eat? What will we drink? What will we wear?' 32 These things dominate the thoughts of unbelievers, but your heavenly Father already knows all your needs. 33 Seek the Kingdom of God[a] above all else, and live righteously, and He will give you everything you need." 34 "So don't worry about tomorrow, for tomorrow will bring its own worries. Today's trouble is enough for today."*

Consider Peter. He was in relationship with Jesus, walked with Him in ministry and needed to pay his taxes. In other words, He was showing up and faithfully staying connected to Jesus, doing everything He needed to be doing at that time in his life. Jesus didn't scold Peter for his need or tell him he should have thought of paying his taxes before he joined them in ministry. Nope. Instead, He supernaturally provided the money Peter needed, in full. Peter was in alignment with the right person, at the right time and that relationship brought him the right resource.

We read in 1 Kings 17:2-16, Elijah was doing what God had called him to do but needed food and drink. God didn't tell him he should have prepared better. He didn't teach him a lesson by letting him go hungry. No! He supernaturally provided for him by using something that made no sense in the natural—ravens. Then, in verse 7, it says that the brook he had been drinking from dried up. Yes, you guessed it. Time to realign for the next part of the assignment. The Lord told him to go to a certain widows' house and instructed that widow to supply Elijah with food. And even in a place of lack—the widow didn't have any bread, only a handful of flour and a little olive oil— God supernaturally provided for Elijah, the widow and her family. Right place, right time, right provision.

And what about Bezalel, the artisan who was tapped by God to build and decorate the Tabernacle of Moses? In Exodus 31, he is described as being both filled with the Spirit of God and skilled in every ability needed to accomplish his assignment. And it's obvious, because of the favor on his life, he was in alignment with God, the leaders in his life and other artisans. So much so that we read in Exodus 36, Bezalel had to go to Moses and ask him to restrain the people from giving because they had already received an abundance of resources for the project. An overflow of provision. When's the last time the bank called you and said you had too much money in the bank and you needed to stop making deposits for a while? And yet, that's the kind of favor Bezalel was walking in. He had all the authority, opportunity and relationships he needed to accomplish his assignment along with an abundant flow of resources. Right place, right time, right provision.

Jesus was clear in Matthew 6:33 NLT when He said, "*Seek the Kingdom of God above all else, and live righteously, and He will give you everything you need.*" Everything means everything. No lack. No need. Not just enough to get by. Everything. God's not a liar. And He's not setting you up just to pull the rug out from under you. He's good. He's got unlimited resources for you. More than enough. And He's ready to give it to you in abundance as you align with Him. Remember, the Bible says in Psalm 84:11 NLT, "*For the LORD God is our sun and our shield. He gives us grace and glory. The LORD will withhold no good thing from those who do what is right.*"

Throughout the whole Biblical narrative, it's clear that God's heart is to bless His children with abundance, not just barely enough to survive. We never see God portrayed as a stingy provider in His Word! Eden was fruitful, fertile and filled with plenty of resources. Even as He was teaching the children of Israel to obey and walk by faith before the New Covenant, there was daily provision to satisfy their needs and a double portion on the sixth day to cover the Sabbath. When Jesus turned the water into wine, there were gallons and gallons, not just a few bottles hidden in the back room. When Jesus instructed the disciples who had been fishing all night to throw their net over to the other side, there were so many fish that it almost caused their nets to break.

And God wants us to operate out of that same generous abundance, too! Just like in the story of the Good Samaritan, where the man who stopped to help his neighbor spared no expense. He ministered to the man on the roadside, took him to a nearby inn and told the innkeeper he'd pay whatever it costs to take care of the man. That's the God we serve! And in the Kingdom, you can both receive His abundant blessings and be a conduit of blessing to others.

I hope you will forever throw out of your mind the idea that God wants to give you just enough to barely get by in order to keep you humble. It's unbiblical hogwash and it's certainly not God's heart for you. He's your good father who will not give you a stone or a snake when you ask for fish or bread (Matthew 7:9-11). He loves you and desires to bless you with good things—more than enough—as you walk with Him.

*As you walk with God, continue to mature in your design and faithfully pursue your assignment, there's no limit to what God will bring into your life— spiritually and in the natural.*

## Aligned to Be a Blessing

Alignment isn't only about being in the right place to receive what we need. It's also about being aligned with God to be a blessing to others. Remember, we have been restored to be an ambassador of transformation to others. Just think of the little boy in John 6 who brought the five loaves and two fish to Jesus. He probably had no idea what would happen that day, but he was willing. He was with Jesus—in the right place and at the right time—and God used what he brought to feed thousands of people in a powerful demonstration of alignment. When we are rightly aligned with Jesus, we will receive all the provision we need in abundance with an overflow left over. And God will use that abundance as a blessing to others. Remember, God's Word says in 2 Corinthians 9:8 NLT *"And God will generously provide all you need. Then you will always have everything you need and plenty left over to share with others."* As you learn to walk in the Kingdom of God as His child, you can trust that you will always have more than enough. More than enough to walk in your unique design, accomplish your God-given assignment, fulfill the desires of your heart and be a pipeline of blessing to others.

While we lived in Asheville, I was privileged to be on the board of directors for one of the largest homeless shelters and recovery ministries in Western North Carolina. As I served, the Lord began to drop an idea into my heart about creating an outside mural for the building. Now, just so you get the picture, we're not talking about a little building. We're talking a huge brick building in a downtown area with major visibility. As I began to imagine this with the Lord, He told me that He wanted my wife and I to underwrite the cost, then gave me a number. A big number. I gulped and then shared it with Tanya. She gulped and then we gave God our "yes". Then as I continued to pray about it, God gave me the beginnings of a design and told me the name of the artist that was supposed to complete the project.

Once I knew we were fully committed to the mural project, I realized I hadn't even asked the director if they wanted a mural for their building. When I approached him, he was overjoyed and said that a mural had always been part of his dream for the center—a public display of God's healing power to the city. More than just meeting the basic needs of those they ministered to, he had a desire to celebrate all Jesus was doing in the lives of the people.

I told him the amount of money we would commit to the project, the design I thought could be a starting point and who I recommended for the project. As we talked, the presence of the Lord was tangible. And later when I reached out to the artist to see if he had an interest in the project and the time in his schedule to create this mural, he immediately agreed. As we worked together on the project, it morphed into not one, but two humongous murals. One on each side of the building and visible from either direction on a main downtown thoroughfare. God provided the additional financial support for the project and it was a huge success. Now every time someone passes that building, they not only see the faces of people who've been transformed, but they also see the miracle working power of Jesus. But it all started with our simple 'yes'.

When you offer what you have to Jesus, He will accelerate and multiply your efforts to the point of overflow. It's a process that happens over time as you faithfully stay in the process with Him.

And you can trust Him even when things don't make sense. As you do, He will position you with the right people, place you in the right place and at the right time provide you every resource and strategy you need to fulfill all God has designed for you to accomplish. Continue to respond in faith—day by day—and you will live a life without limits. That's what it means to walk in Kingdom alignment.

But without love, it can turn into a big mess. And that's why the last part of God's IDEAL Framework is Love.

# Chapter 9

*Living from Love*

Depending on which translation of the Bible you prefer, the Bible mentions love anywhere between 300-600+ times! So, if we were going to pick one precept that would be the glue that holds everything together in the Kingdom and in our lives—love is that precept. But why is love so important? Because without it, our natural tendency is to self-protect and perform. Protecting ourselves from things we think might harm us. Performing for God and others, giving them the version we think they want to see. Both are a mirage of security and connection that leaves us empty and wanting more.

Left unfilled, the empty places of our heart will be drawn to actions and feelings that promise to satisfy, but never do. Actions that innocently come from a desire to avoid pain can soon turn into coping mechanisms, addictions, or sin with unhealthy consequences. This is the human condition apart from God's Love. If we don't operate from the Love of God, we look for something or someone else to fill our emptiness. Other "lovers" who promise a quick fix to mend the broken places and soothe our pain.

## Rooted and Grounded in Love

If we don't let God define who we are, by default we allow others to define us. These replacements for the Love of God become the place we receive life, affirmation, fulfillment and identity. What matters to us, motivates and moves us. And what matters is determined by what's in our hearts. That's why the Love of God must be our foundation for living.

Without being, "rooted and grounded in love" as the Bible says in Ephesians 3:17, we'll never know or experience the fullness of God in our lives. But this beautiful section of scripture in Ephesians describes God's ideal best.

*"I pray that from His glorious, unlimited resources He will empower you with inner strength through His Spirit. 17 Then Christ will make His home in your hearts as you trust in Him. Your roots will grow down into God's Love and keep you strong. 18 And may you have the power to understand, as all God's people should, how wide, how long, how high, and how deep His Love is. 19 May you experience the Love of Christ, though it is too great to understand fully. Then you will be made complete with all the fullness of life and power that comes from God. 20 Now all glory to God, who is able, through His mighty power at work within us, to accomplish infinitely more than we might ask or think."* Ephesians 3:16-20 NLT

We were designed to live empowered by the unlimited resources of God. As we embrace our connection with Christ, our hearts grow deep roots in His love. This increases our capacity to grow strong in the Lord and accomplish all He's called us to in the Kingdom. It's the Love of God that completes and fulfills us, not our striving. We can accomplish infinitely more when the Love of God is operating in and through us when we live from the position of being already loved rather than performing for His Love.

God's Love is meant to be our life source. From that place, all things are possible. But if you've never experienced the Love of God, it's impossible to live from it, much less extend it to others. Left to our own devices, we seek life from other sources and end up striving to accomplish the fruit of a Spirit-led life. That's what the enemy does. He shows us a legitimate desire, then falsely promises us an expedited way – a counterfeit - to get there apart from God's plan. These misguided attempts often lead to sin, which the Bible defines as "missing the mark". Satan loves to get our heart pointed in the wrong direction.

## Sin is a Love Issue

At its root, every sin is a love issue. Here's why: sin is rooted and grounded in disconnection from God. Since the beginning of time, the enemy has sown doubt into man's heart about God's Love for us. He did it with Adam and Eve and he's still doing it today. The seeds of doubt and deception are sown in our hearts in a myriad of ways. Through trauma and wounds we receive from others, the result of unhealthy things we've done, or simply because the enemy wants to take us out through no fault of our own. But here's the bottom line. When we believe the enemy's lies and no longer trust God's intentions, we disconnect our hearts from Him. And even though our desire for love is a valid, God-given need, we begin to look to people, possessions, positions, or performances for love and

*An inability to receive love will always result in separation from God and others.*

validation—anything to fill the void. But these things can never satisfy. And, when they don't, it draws us further away from God and further into sin.

This disconnection happens so slowly it is often unnoticeable. But over time, it causes a calloused desperation. Our empty search reinforces our disconnection from God. Eventually, we go into self-protection mode and look to escape the pain of life by any means possible. Even though we want to love and receive love, we're unable to because of our disappointing experiences. Our hearts become hardened, unable to give or receive real love.

An inability to receive love will always result in separation from God and others. Things like social isolation, emotional distancing, seeking pleasure over pain and unhealthy coping mechanisms can seem like self-protection, but ultimately, they separate us from the very thing we need the most—a connection with God and others. When we rely on those things more than God, it deepens our connection to an illegitimate source and we end up settling for temporary fixes instead of lasting love.

Sex, substance abuse, food, performance, media-binging—the list goes on. We end up going down roads we never thought we would because of the void in our heart. Seemingly innocent self-medicating habits turn into addictions. Our world gets darker and more isolated, which is the enemy's plan all along. A vicious circle of self-sabotage separates us from God, others and our authentic self, stopping us from living in our unique design or accomplishing our Kingdom assignment.

This is why I believe, at its root, every sin issue is a LOVE issue.

## Ongoing Encounter with Love

God wants us to encounter His unreserved and unconditional love in such a way that we are forever transformed. Not just once, but every day. When we cultivate an ongoing encounter with God, the roots of our heart grow deep in Him, creating a connection with God that reveals the lies of the enemy and dispels the draw of sin. It establishes our identity in Christ, builds internal confidence and empowers us to engage in life-giving relationships with others based on who God says we are. Operating from any other place is a recipe for disaster.

We began our journey together talking about the foundational nature of identity and how it shapes the inner framework of our heart and creates the lens through which we see God, others, the world and the opportunities we encounter. But that can't just be a cognitive exercise of simply memorizing scripture and saying positive words. You'll drive yourself crazy seeking out the latest life hack from every self-help guru on social media. True Kingdom transformation in our lives cannot happen without an ongoing encounter with the deep, tangible Love of God. Otherwise, we'll jump right back into striving or performing.

## Without Love

When Paul taught about the spiritual gifts and supernatural tools we have access to as Kingdom people in 1 Corinthians 12, he ends the chapter by saying in verse 31, "*So you should earnestly desire the most helpful gifts. But now let me show you a way of life that is best of all.*" (NLT) That "best" way of life is love. We can't walk in the fullness of our identity, design, assignment and gifts if we are not rooted and grounded in God's Love. Without love, we'll miss the mark even with the best of intentions.

In 1 Corinthians 13, Paul spends the whole chapter explaining why our exploits for God, even using the gifts God gave us, are worthless without love as our motivating factor. That's always been such a reality check for me. Without love, anything I do—even the good things He has asked me to do through the gifts and graces He gave me—becomes an annoying gong or clanging cymbal to God as Paul mentions in I Corinthians 13:1. Off course and distracted, we will miss the mark.

## Heart Strangely Warmed

I'm reminded of the story of John Wesley, revivalist and founder of Methodism who had an incredible impact on his generation and beyond. After years of working in professional ministry, he hungered for more of God, but didn't know what more looked like. Consequently, he found himself in a series of divine appointments, culminating at Aldersgate in May of 1738 where he heard a reading of Luther's preface to the Epistle to the Romans. Wesley found his heart "strangely warmed" and later described that as the moment He trusted in Jesus for his salvation. And it all started with a deep longing for more and a life-changing encounter with the Love of God.

Like Wesley, it's possible to operate from a place of religious passion, duty and obligation yet be void of real intimacy with Jesus. But, when we are fueled by an ongoing encounter with the Holy

Spirit, everything changes! We experience fruitfulness and fulfillment like never before. In fact, the years after Wesley's Aldersgate salvation experience were his most influential for the Kingdom. Love made the difference.

## He's Looking for Your Heart

As much as I've tried to explain how the Kingdom works and our role as co-laborers with Christ, let me be clear so there's absolutely no confusion.

> *God isn't looking for our productivity. He wants our hearts.*

And, He knows when He has our heart, He has the opportunity to lead us into everything He designed for us before the very foundation of the world.

God has graciously invited us into His story but it can only be accomplished by His Spirit, not our striving. As I mentioned before in the introduction of this book, like Paul, we are still on the journey of pressing toward the goal. We don't always understand the way things happen or the timeframe in which they occur, but we can rest assured—as we cooperate with God, His will is being accomplished in and through our life.

When we cultivate an intimate relationship with Him, co-laboring with the Holy Spirit's vision, our faith grows—enabling us to walk in confidence and cease our striving. Jesus clarifies this in Matthew 7:22-23, when He said, "*On judgment day many will say to me, 'Lord! Lord! We prophesied in your name and cast out demons in your name and performed many miracles in your name.'* [23] *But I will reply, 'I never knew you. Get away from me, you who break God's laws.'*" (NLT)

Again, we can do a lot of seemingly great things for God but if it doesn't come out of a place of real connection and love, it is of no lasting value. And worse, it can keep us from a real relationship with God.

## Anchored in Love

Love must be our anchor for everything—the pivot point from which everything originates. Our starting motivation and our end result. Otherwise, every desire, vision, action and response we undertake will be anchored in self-protection, self-gratification or performance.

Anchored in the Love of God, we can safely risk without fear of shame, hurt or loss. We can walk in confidence because we know, ultimately, we have nothing to lose. Not only in our individual life, but also within the community. Even though God's Love rarely makes sense to your natural mind—calling us to risk and trust in the face of fear—it is the foundation for Kingdom living.

Imagine how different the world would look if a unified Church operated from the Love of God. How vastly different it would look compared to what we see now. Instead of leading with agendas and issues, we would lead with love and concern for individuals. Instead of seeking to strengthen our position, we would seek to be ambassadors of healing and reconciliation. Instead of trying to make sure our point of view was heard, respected and adopted as the law of the land, we would build relationships that become the breeding ground for transformation.

## Beyond Agenda

Regardless of your affiliation, no political party or idealistic movement is entirely rooted in love. And most don't even pretend to be. They are rooted in an unadulterated desire for power, money and influence. They seek to control and dominate the narrative. They want to see their preferences implemented and are willing to create unholy alliances to see it happen. And when it no longer serves them, they turn on each other without loyalty. Their agenda has nothing to do with the Love of God. To think otherwise is to be deceived.

Jesus had a vision for societal transformation, but it had nothing to do with attaining political power. It had everything to do with pouring His Love out on the cross and by extension, through His children. Jesus resisted political domination, but was a passionate advocate for justice. His model of societal change was, and still is, transforming individuals through God's Love, then joining them together as His Body on the earth—to see His Kingdom come and His will be done on earth as it is in heaven.

When the early church laid aside their own agenda and learned to walk in love as members of the Body of Christ—empowered by the

Holy Spirit—whole cities were shaken. One spontaneous sermon and thousands were saved. A few letters sent to fledgling churches yielded generational, worldwide influence resulting in millions upon millions coming to the Lord. That's how the Kingdom worked then and it's how it works today. As we cooperate with Him, we experience His multiplying, accelerating and transforming power flowing through us.

Without love, everything else is a powerplay of preference. A form of godliness that denies God's power. It turns the church into a bloated political show concerned with its own comfort and reputation rather than a humble family of believers committed to Spirit-birthed transformation who are willing to lay down their nets, take up their cross and follow Jesus.

If God has called you into the political realm to make a difference in the nation you live in, that's wonderful! We need godly men and women serving in areas of leadership, but not leaders who have their own agenda. Authentic Kingdom influence must always be marked by a humble boldness. Relationship and reconciliation bathed in love. Life-giving solutions that also serve the marginalized and hurting. Uncommon wisdom that comes from Heaven, not just good intentions.

## Unforgiveness Inhibits Love

It's vitally important that love is the lens through which we choose to see ourselves and God, because that determines how we see everyone else. If we don't love ourselves as God loves us, we'll find ourselves in relationships filled with caveats and conditions, unable to love or receive healthy love and affirmation from others. A love deficit discolors our view of everything. But encountering the Love of God clarifies.

A significant part of what often blocks a person's ability to love themselves is unforgiveness. When you refuse to forgive another person, it eats away at you and causes a bitter root of judgement. And when you sow judgement of others, that's what you reap in your own life. Unfortunately, the only person that hurts is you. Most of the time, the other person isn't even thinking about the issue that you're still so upset about.

My parents divorced when I was 16. It was the summer between my junior and senior year in high school. While I was glad there'd be a stop to the constant fighting between them, there was deep, unresolved pain in me that I had no ability to process in a healthy way. Consequently, I stuffed it, deep.

After walking through some difficult years and holding unforgiveness in my heart toward my dad, the Lord gently reminded me he was the only dad I had and if I wanted a relationship with him, then I was going to have to be the one to reach out. But I didn't want to. I was deeply hurt and still very angry. But as I gave God my "yes" and slowly began to reach out to my dad, our relationship started to heal. It wasn't all roses, but I extended forgiveness and God began to open our hearts. Over time, the Lord restored our relationship to better than it was before.

## The Power of Forgiveness

Forgiving my dad did several things for me. It released me from the judgments I was making against him so I didn't have to experience those things in my life. It freed me from the pain I was holding inside from all those years of family turmoil so I could walk in freedom. It gave me the ability to see him through a lens of love, mercy and compassion. And it allowed me to break a cycle of trauma and unforgiveness in our family so my son didn't have to experience the effects of that in his life. Had I not forgiven my dad, God's best for my life would have been severely thwarted.

As a part of the forgiveness process, I also had to intentionally forgive myself. Unknowingly, I had blamed myself for the trauma I experienced as a young man and it's resulting unhealthy patterns of living. My loving heavenly Father restored my heart as I threw off my false responsibility and fell into the arms of Jesus. I laid down my old, wounded identity and picked up my new identity in Christ. Forgiveness made all the difference.

## No More Autopilot

Life is busy and often overwhelming. It can be tempting to think that living the Christian life will work itself out automatically. Kind of like thinking those old wounds and places of unforgiveness we've been carrying around for years will just heal themselves. But the Kingdom doesn't work like that. We can't simply flip the autopilot switch and hope for the best—though that's how most Christians do life. Time does not heal all unresolved wounds. It just doesn't. It only covers them with years of scar tissue making the healing process much more difficult than if we just dealt with the issue and moved on. Even if we never get a perfect resolution with the other person, we can forgive them and move on with our lives. We must—for our own wellbeing.

Loving ourselves, God and the people we daily encounter doesn't happen automatically. It must become a habit we cultivate. And nobody does it perfectly. We're all in process. But we must determine in our heart to press toward the goal of love. Otherwise, we will take the path of least resistance.

## Living Unchecked

You might be like me in that I don't normally go looking for conflict. Truth be known, I like to avoid it. And that often results in me avoiding situations I should address. It also creates a tendency in me to allow my emotions to go unchecked. Instead of responding to life with intention and purposeful love, I allow my autopilot to kick in. Unfortunately, then I mistake interruptions and inconveniences as something to avoid rather than opportunities for a love encounter.

I can remember one time my son, Cameron, who was a young teen at the time, was having a particularly hard day. His response to the stress in his life unfortunately pushed all my buttons. Instead of asking the Lord how I could have responded to Cameron with love or comfort, I responded with very hurtful words. So much so, Tanya turned to me, stunned. Cameron was hurt and I was frustrated by my stupid response and lack of empathy. Thankfully, after things calmed down, I apologized to Cameron and made amends. But I missed a moment to live from love.

## Overlooked Opportunities

It's also easy to overlook the divine appointments and supernatural intersections the Lord has for us. Years ago, I had the opportunity to be on the podcast of an extremely well-known Christian leader.

Consequently, it was heard around the world and I still get comments from people who said that is where they first heard of me.

One day, a woman came into my art studio and mentioned she had heard me on that podcast. It wasn't the first time I'd heard that, so I nodded politely and engaged in some light small talk. She then told me she and her family had just moved to the area to plant a church and were looking for Kingdom people to connect with. I had heard this before, so I gave her a nice smile, spoke a few surface level words and sent her on her way. I was busy and she was just one of many people that came through the studio that day.

Years later, while speaking at a church in our area, my wife and I met a couple before the service who led their inner healing ministry. Long story short, we immediately connected on a heart level and decided we wanted to get to know each other more. We went to dinner that week and started one of the most meaningful friendships we've ever had. It was like we'd known each other for years. It was only after getting to know each other that my friend shared she was the woman I'd met in the studio years earlier. We had a good laugh because I didn't remember the details. But, as I think back on it now, I wonder what we missed as couples in the Kingdom. What could we have experienced had I chosen to respond with a heart to connect with His Love, rather than my own busyness? Thankfully, there's no shame and we all had a laugh! But the bottom line is this: it takes intentionality to walk in love. We must choose to look through the eyes of Jesus, listen through the ears of Jesus, feel through the heart of Jesus. It doesn't happen automatically.

*Our motives matter
because everything
we do flows
from who we are.*

As Paul reminds us in 1 Corinthians 16: 14 ESV, "*Let all that you do be done in love.*" The permeating Love of God alone is the foundation for everything in the Kingdom. Without it, you will always default to the path of least resistance.

## Motives Matter

Proverbs 21:2 ESV says, "*Every man's way is right in his own eyes, but the Lord weighs the heart.*" That's why it's important to ask the Holy Spirit to search our hearts when we meet with Him each day. Not as a self-hating, navel gazing habit, looking for a demon under every rock or constantly feeling like we don't measure up. No! We ask because we know we are God's beloved child and the searching of our hearts by the Holy Spirit is part of our refinement and maturity process in the Kingdom. And as we ask, Holy Spirit will reveal the things keeping us from receiving and giving His Love.

He reveals barriers in our walk with the Lord because He loves us and wants us to become more like Jesus. Conformed to His image as God designed and destined us to be. When we operate outside of Love's foundation, everything we produce is hay and stubble and will be consumed in His presence when we stand before Him. Our motives matter because everything we do flows from who we are.

If you're a performer, then what matters most is how others see and respond to you. In that place, your motive will always be to do whatever you need to do to get the response you desire—working hard to create a successful and perfect life to impress others. You'll lean toward exaggeration and make yourself and anything you're a part of more than it really is so others will think you've got it all together.

If you see yourselves as a victim, self-preservation and protection is what matters most. You'll bounce back and forth between avoiding conflict, reducing your pain and staying hidden—to manipulating others to meet your legitimate physical, emotional and relationship needs in an unhealthy way. You'll tend to embrace self-pity and reject thoughts worth celebrating, fixating on past negative experiences which keep you paralyzed and unable to move forward. You'll blame others for what you have experienced rather than take the responsibility for your healing journey.

If you're a narcissist, what matters most to you is image and power. You are motivated by personal pleasure, image, control and self-protection and see yourself as the center of your own universe. You consider yourself first and have little empathy for others. You constantly seek attention approval and validation from others instead of from God, the way it was intended.

## Dismantling False Identities

Usually at the bottom of each of our false identities is a deep underlying fear of being exposed as a fake, a fraud, an imposter. We fear that if people really knew who we were on the inside, they would reject us, leaving us all alone. And for most people, that potential rejection is simply unbearable. A core strategy of every wounded framework is a desire to control. People, situations, impressions—the list goes on. Why? To protect our image, reduce our pain or increase our pleasure. Once again, placing ourselves at the center.

The only truly lasting way to transform our interior motives is to experience an ongoing encounter with the Love of God. To be fully known, seen, accepted, forgiven, celebrated and loved. This transformation happens in several ways: through worship and cultivating an ongoing awareness of the presence of God, intentionally renewing our mind with God's Word, being in life-giving community with other believers and through regularly taking an honest inventory regarding the motives of our hearts.

## Search Me, O God

Let's be honest. We all tend to lie to ourselves about what's really going on inside our heart. In Psalm 139:23-24, David asked God to help him—"*Search me, O God, and know my heart; Try me, and know my anxieties; And see if there is any wicked way in me, And lead me in the way everlasting.*" (NKJV) Just like David, we need to allow God to search out our motives. There's no magic formula, but here's what I would encourage you to do.

First, take time in a quiet place to awaken your awareness of God's presence. Remember, He's present in you now through the power of the Holy Spirit. You don't have to beg God to show up. Thank God for His presence and His Love for you. Maybe take a little time to worship with music or just enjoy the silence of the moment. Remind yourself what God has said about you according to His Word.

Once you feel loved and affirmed by the Father, invite the Holy Spirit to reveal the motives of your heart. Maybe there's a certain situation you're walking through, a struggle or difficulty. Invite Him into the places where fear and pain are causing you anxiety. Listen with the ears of your heart. Look with the eyes of your redeemed imagination. Ask God to reveal if there are any negative coping patterns, habits or recurring thoughts you may have adopted that don't agree with His best for your life. Then, ask Him to heal the broken places of your heart and help you live from a place of love, not fear.

As He walks you through this process, use the 5R's for Renewing Your Mind I shared with you earlier in the book to recognize the enemy's lies. Repent of places where you've agreed with them and replace them with the truth of God's Word. As you make this a part of your regular time with the Lord, your life will be transformed and conformed into the image of Christ.

## Love Changes Everything

When you begin to cultivate an ongoing encounter with the Love of God, your perspective will shift from yourself to seeing life through God's eyes—a place of design and destiny rather than brokenness and inability. You'll see others through the eyes of compassion and interruptions as unexpected opportunities to release love. As you spend time in God's Word and presence, your desires align with the Father's. You become like the one you behold. Favor will be released in your life. Not because God is in a good mood and decided to bless you, but because you came into alignment with what He was already doing in the Kingdom. And finally, you'll see an abundance of fruit in your life. The things you do will matter and have lasting Kingdom impact for you and those around you.

## You Never Know Who's Watching

Years ago, I walked through a difficult situation with a colleague. This person was in the middle of a tough transition and I was still learning how to lead and love well. Unfortunately, that led to a lot of emotion, frustration and eventually anger between us. What had been a fruitful relationship spiraled into turmoil. As the difficulty became public and other people could see what was going on, I had a choice. Would I respond to the situation in anger or honor. It was not an easy decision.

I chose honor in both public and private settings. Even though I had played a part in the difficulty, I felt angry, hurt and rejected. I had to ask the Lord to search my heart and help me release those things to Him so I could walk in His Love and freedom. As I did, the weight of the situation lifted and a refreshing wind flowed through my life and business.

A couple of years passed and I was invited to keynote at a Christian conference in another country. Though I had known the person who invited me for some time, He was much closer to my former colleague than he was me, but I was honored to be invited, nonetheless. We had some time to visit before I spoke and he shared something I found to be surprising. He told me the reason he had invited me to speak at this conference was because of how I walked through that relational difficulty with our mutual friend. You see, he was watching how I responded in those moments and it made an impact in his life. That's the power of choosing to walk in love.

## Jesus Operated from Love

The Gospels clearly show us that Jesus operated from love. He said, "if you've seen me, you've seen the Father." And since God is Love, we can definitively say that as Jesus walked the earth and dwelled among humanity, He was both the image and demonstration of love. He was a walking love encounter. But in His humanity, He did some practical things we can implement in our own lives to connect with the Love of the Father more fully.

Jesus spent time alone with the Father in prayer and worship. He did this to reconnect to the Source of all life. All throughout the Gospels, Jesus is described as pulling away from the demands of people and ministry to reconnect and recharge. I love the passage in John 5:19 when Jesus responds to the religious leaders about the accusation of breaking the sabbath, "So," Jesus explained, "*I tell you the truth, the Son can do nothing by himself. He does only what He sees the Father doing. Whatever the Father does, the Son also does. For the Father loves the Son and shows Him everything He is doing. In fact, the Father will show Him how to do even greater works than healing this man. Then you will truly be astonished.*" (NLT) In other words, Jesus was saying they hadn't seen anything yet! Everything He did came out of the love relationship He had with His Father. And there was more to come—things He would do that would blow them away.

Jesus modeled what living from love looked like before His disciples and everywhere He encountered people. Throughout the Gospels, we see Him move seamlessly with the Father, operating from love, not obligation or a desire to do something for the Father out of His own zeal. When Jesus saw people in difficult situations—He was moved with compassion. He wept. He engaged in conversation. He invested in relationship with the unlikeliest of people. Jesus saw every person and situation as an opportunity to release life and connect with the Father's heart for that person. Not for His own glory, but so the Kingdom would come and the Father's will would be done on earth as it is in heaven.

He even demonstrated love and honor in little situations that didn't seem like a big deal. Like in John 2 when Jesus's mother asks Him to turn some water into wine at a wedding because they were running out. Even though it wasn't time for Him to begin His public ministry, Jesus had a choice: to refuse his mom because she was asking Him to do something before it was time, or to respond in love. He chose love which honored His mom and blessed others.

*Sometimes you have to set aside what makes sense in the natural to respond in the supernatural.*

When Jesus encountered the woman at the well in John 4, He had another choice. He could have responded to her with counsel or stern rebuke, accusation or even frustration. But He chose to see her through the eyes of love. Just like He did all throughout the Gospels. He saw her, responded with empathy and love, revealed her heart and offered her new life. He chose to administer life and speak love in a situation that most people would have ignored or used for their own benefit.

In the Garden of Gethsemane, when Simon Peter cut off the ear of a Roman soldier, Jesus had a choice. To respond in anger and frustration, or to respond in love. In an extremely tense moment— He chose love. He healed the ear of his enemy and spoke truth to His disciple. Sometimes a love response looks like healing an enemy and sometimes it looks like speaking a hard truth to a friend.

## Transformed by an Encounter with Love

When the Love of God matters most, it motivates and moves us from a wounded, self-serving place to a healthy place. As we live from a place of ongoing encounter with the Love of God, we will be changed. But here's even better news: those we encounter will be changed too! Not because we have it all together, but because we carry the life-giving presence of God which overflows onto those around us.

Consider Paul. He lived many years motivated by religion and control but was completely out of step with the new reality of the Kingdom. Until he had a love encounter with God in Acts 9. A love that knew everything he had ever done. Transformed by love on that Damascus Road: his name was changed, his destiny was altered and he started walking in Kingdom fruitfulness like never before.

And what would cause someone like Mary Magdalene in John 12 to come into a meeting and begin washing the feet of Jesus with extremely expensive perfume? Certainly not religious obligation. It was potentially embarrassing and even scandalous for her to be there. But she had encountered the Love of God as a follower of Jesus and was forever changed. The lens of God's Love changes what you see as needed, necessary and possible.

The same invitation is being offered to you and me today. The choice to love others because He first loved us. Will we live from God's Love and resist the temptation to see the faults of everyone? Will we choose instead to see others through the eyes of love? Choose love even when we feel others deserve punishment? Will we give up our need to always prove our point, believe the best in others and seek reconciliation before confrontation? As we live from God's Love, His power will flow through us and to us in abundance— transforming us into a conduit for the life of God.

## A New Lens for Life

I have an astigmatism in my left eye and it's significant. So much so, the eye doctor has to bring out the heavy-duty box of lenses when creating my prescription. As he offers me a different lens, asking if this one or that is better here or here, my vision becomes clearer and I realize I've been looking at everything through a warped view. Although it was my natural eye, it wasn't telling me the truth about what I was seeing.

The same is true with how we perceive life, others, situations and our opportunities. Our perspective and truth, is naturally skewed. Just because we've always seen things one way doesn't mean they are correct or God's best way to see them. That's simply become our normal. And our normal informs and shapes our responses to life.

But in the Kingdom, God wants His normal to become our normal. He wants to fundamentally transform our responses from fear to faith. It happens as we learn to live from love.

When we respond in fear, self-protection is always the root. We think we can't do "this" or "that" because "this" or "that" might happen. Love doesn't fear. In fact, the Bible says in 1 John 4:18 NKJV, "*There is no fear in love; but perfect love casts out fear, because fear involves torment. But he who fears has not been made perfect in love.*"

When we respond out of lack and desperation, provision issues are usually the root. We think we can't give because then we won't have enough for ourselves, or we can't pursue a dream because we don't have enough money to invest in ourselves. But love doesn't lack. It isn't desperate. Remember, the Bible says in Psalm 34:9-10 NIV, *"Fear the LORD, you His holy people, for those who fear Him lack nothing. The lions may grow weak and hungry, but those who seek the LORD lack no good thing."*

## Seeing Through a New Lens

We can respond in faith, with confident expectation, when our life is rooted in God's Love. When we declare, "I can do all things through Christ who gives me strength", we are extending our faith. In Him, we always have more than enough. In Christ we are protected, strengthened and provided for. We can do whatever God asks us to do because there's always abundant provision and favor for the call.

When we see life through the lens of fear and lack, all we see is impossibility, inability and worst-case scenarios. We worry and stress people will take advantage of us and doubt the motives of others instead of believing the best. We hold grudges instead of freely offering forgiveness and setting both parties free. In our desire to remain in control, we measure out joy and emotion. With that mindset, it's impossible to please God. Why? Because that's not operating from a place of faith, rooted and grounded in love.

But when we see life through the lens of love, we are easily moved with compassion. We can step out in faith as the Holy Spirit nudges us even when it doesn't make sense in the natural. We can confidently give a word to someone we don't know even when it feels risky. And, we can forgive and move through difficulty—believing the best of others by faith—because we trust more in God than in man.

Living from love changes everything. It enables us to see life's challenges and opportunities through the lens of God's power rather than our own inability or inadequacy. From the perspective of being seated with Christ rather than desperate for His intervention. Life comes into view the way God designed. Our old, warped view becomes crystal clear. Love frees us to do everything with confidence, to be everything and have everything God designed us for without the self-imposed limitations of fear.

When we feel those old familiar responses rising up in our hearts, and they will, we need to ask ourselves if we are living from love or from lack, need or fear. Resist what feels natural in the flesh and make an intentional choice to live from love. As we do, it will become our normal. His Love makes the difference. This is the process of sanctification: choosing to love by God's grace, through faith and being transformed by Him in the process.

Now that we've unpacked each of the five principles in God's IDEAL design framework, I want to turn our attention toward how we can implement this in our everyday lives. Instead of living on a revival rollercoaster, up one minute and down the next, we can cultivate an atmosphere of continual breakthrough that becomes our normal operating procedure.

# Chapter 10

*Cultivating an Atmosphere of Breakthrough*

The first man to be anointed King over Israel was Saul. He was the total package. Or so it seemed. He was from a loving, wealthy family, handsome, tall, strong and a valiant warrior. Saul even operated in the prophetic, as seen in 1 Samuel 10:9. Who better to lead a nation than someone with all this gifting? In fact, if you wanted to create a perfect leader profile, this just might be a great list of attributes from which to start.

Some might say Saul was the ideal King for Israel. But even though Saul was talented and anointed by the prophet Samuel to be King, he struggled to walk out God's best for his life. Was it because God didn't love Saul? Absolutely not. It was because even though Saul was talented, anointed and in a position of authority, he refused to allow the Lord to refine him where it was needed. He refused what would have made him thrive in the position God had placed him. And the enemy took advantage of it. Unfortunately, it became his downfall.

## Satan's Recurring Strategy

This is the all-to-common strategy of the enemy. Take someone who is talented, called, anointed and in a position of influence—then use their weaknesses of character to bring them down. A mentor of mine shared with me the old adage that goes, "*Your talent will take you where your character can't keep you.*" And how true that is. In Saul's case, the enemy used his impatience and need to take matters into his own hands to lure him into sin (1 Samuel 13). Saul's refusal to be refined by God led to his crazed insecurity and ultimately, to the loss of his throne.

Just like God, the enemy has an ideal plan for our lives. And it's to lie, confuse, steal, kill and destroy. In every case, the enemy sees our potential and creates scenarios in and around our lives to cause fear and harm to us and those we love. He then uses these situations to torment us and to cause us to live in fear and frustration. Fear and anxiety become a prison that paralyzes and keeps us from stepping into all God has called us to in the Kingdom. When these situations are left unresolved, they become a repeating pattern of self-sabotage.

Satan has a specific attack strategy for each person. And in every case, he goes after our identity, design, expansion, alignment and love. These are our places of power and influence in God's IDEAL plan for us. This is where everything we think, believe and do flows from. If he can get us off course in one of these areas, he knows he has an opportunity to take us down—one fall leading to the next like dominos. Here's how it often works.

## Satan Attacks Identity

Satan attacks our identity first because if he can get us to doubt the goodness of God and who we are in the Kingdom, he knows that will affect everything else in a negative manner. He attacks our design, causing us to second guess our uniqueness and destroys our healthy self-image. He attacks our opportunities for expansion by throwing fiery darts of doubt and fear that psych us out. He places frustrations and temptation in our way, distracting us from fulfilling our God-given assignment. He uses our areas of sin, weakness and woundedness as doorways to access our heart and takes advantage of our negative thinking and living patterns based in our old, unredeemed identity. He tempts us to act and respond out of self-preservation, protection, jealousy and fear rather than from a place of love and trust. And every attack is custom made to keep us from living in God's IDEAL.

## Your Greatest Struggle

I've discovered that our greatest area of struggle often reveals the uniqueness of our calling and its potential impact. That's why the enemy works overtime to sabotage us there. But if we learn to recognize this demonic strategy, it can become a way to further clarify who we are and all that God's called us to in the Kingdom.

For example, I discovered a pattern in my life where the enemy was using my immaturity against me, specifically in my design as an exhorter—one who was created to be bright, shiny, encouraging, inspiring and leading the way for others. Over and over, I was set up to fail. He would wait until I was in a place of influence and then cause me to stumble through an immature response or sin. But over the years, I started to recognize this pattern. Since I wanted to overcome and not be overcome by these attacks, I sought a way to change the pattern of defeat into a pathway to breakthrough. I confessed my struggles to the Lord and asked Him to give me a revelation as to how I could mature in these areas. My fears, defeats and moments of weakness showed me where God wanted to strengthen me and where my anointing was. And as I confessed, God gave me the grace to grow and mature so I could walk in the fullness of my design. He wants to do the same for you.

Early on in ministry, after serving in several different churches, I noticed I kept encountering the same type of person. Different city, different church, but the same person—full of opinions and not afraid to share them with me. Every time I encountered them, I became extremely irritated. Who did they think they were to critique what I was doing in my job! Finally, after sharing this frustration with my wife, we concluded that God was trying to teach me something. Instead of responding in frustration and continuing to go around this mountain every few months, I started asking the Lord how to deal with people I found to be difficult. He started giving me grace and strategy to mature in this area. He knew my calling required I learn to maturely walk with people that got on my nerves. As I matured in this area and refused to let this interpersonal dynamic control me, I met fewer and fewer of those people along the way. Lesson learned. Spirit-led maturity made the difference.

I don't know what your struggle looks like. It may be pride and insecurity that masks a need for confidence in Christ. Maybe it's an overwhelming desire for money and success masking a need for total dependence on God as your provider. Or perhaps it could it be lust and sexual desires that are outside of God's original design, masking a deep need for authentic love and intimacy. Whatever your struggle is, it reveals an area God wants to go deeper with you. An area where significant work is needed so He can establish great authority in your life. But until you deal with whatever it is, He will continue to allow those same situations to keep coming up. Not to destroy you, but to give you an opportunity to receive healing and bring you into maturity.

## Getting Off the Rollercoaster

For most of my life, I would go from disaster to disaster, crying out to God for breakthrough. I'd screw things up and then need His help to get me out of it again. Though I'd promise if He helped me this time to never screw up again, months later, I'd be back in the same mess. I saw God as my constant Rescuer and the one to get me out of a bad situation when things didn't go my way. Unfortunately, I didn't understand God was also my Keeper and my Strength. My Restorer and Help. In other words, I didn't have to wait for a crisis in my life to cry out for God's help. I could reach out to Him moment by moment. I could cultivate an atmosphere of breakthrough that allowed me to walk through life and all its difficulties in the power of His presence. Discovering that changed everything.

It takes intentionality to cultivate an atmosphere of breakthrough. An atmosphere where we move from glory to glory. This doesn't mean we will never face another difficulty. No! It simply means when we do make a mistake or go through a difficulty, we're not back at ground zero. We don't have to prove our love for God to get back in His good graces or convince Him to forgive us. An atmosphere of breakthrough is one where we are rooted and grounded in God's Love, confident in His unwavering Love. It's an atmosphere where we see our life as a journey with Christ rather than a performance. When we live in an atmosphere of breakthrough, we quickly get back up after a fall and keep moving.

It's really easy to get excited about what God has promised. People will often shout, sing and dance all the way to the altar for a miracle moment or impartation. But when it's time to respond in faith to the opportunities His promise offers, the excitement fades. The excuses emerge. Unbelief rises. People who once shouted out thanks for the promises, shrink back.

Over the years I've noticed, it's a small percentage of people that are willing to do what it takes to see change happen in their life, no matter how easy you make it for them. I would estimate under 5%. People often love prophetic words but not the agreement and faith it takes to walk them into existence. However, the good news is, you don't have to wait on change to happen. The only thing standing in your way is you. Start walking, trust God and keep moving.

## The Power of Double-Mindedness

A foundational part of that intentionality is based on what we believe. And to build a stable, strong foundation, we must set our minds firmly on God's truth. Otherwise, we will be double-minded and unstable (James 1:5-8), trying to hold two opposite things as true in our mind, serving two masters (Matthew 6:24), which is impossible.

Think about the Israelites in the Old Testament. Why in the world did it take them forty years to get to the land God promised them when most scholars believe the journey should have taken less than two weeks? One could easily assume unbelief and that's partly true. But I think it was more likely double-mindedness. It's not necessarily that they didn't want to believe God's promises were true. They just had a stronger belief in the difficulties they faced rather than God's faithfulness to bring them through. Instead of choosing one, they wavered between the two.

Instead of taking the blessing, bounty and benefits of the land God had promised them, they waited on God to do it for them. Doing so cost them a very high price. Wavering between belief and unbelief delayed and distracted them from God's best. And for many, it prevented them from ever entering the promised land.

*Fear is simply faith that's directed toward something other than God.*

But in the Kingdom, faith is belief pointed toward what God's Word says is possible combined with the conviction to act on it. Everyone has a measure of faith. But not everyone points it toward God's Word. When we point our faith to what we can see, touch, or feel in the natural and trust our experience and the opinions of others over the truth of what God has spoken, it creates a never-ending movie in our mind. And since our brain is wired to create pathways and solutions toward the dominant narrative going on in our heart and mind, it moves us toward a result that does not align with God's best.

Unfortunately, the Israelites aren't the only ones guilty of a defeating mindset. This is a recurring theme throughout the Bible. God promises to overwhelm people with His Love and goodness if they will just believe. And in return, His people doubt Him, come up with another plan that makes more sense in the natural and vacillate between the two opportunities. Then when things go bad, cry out to Him for rescue. Sound familiar? It's the human condition apart from a renewed mind in Christ. Like Jesus said in Matthew 5:37 NKJV, "...*let your 'Yes' be 'Yes,' and your 'No,' 'No.' For whatever is more than these is from the evil one.*"

## How You See Yourself Matters

Many Christians prefer to live in survival-mode, needing continual rescue rather than living by faith, believing in the possibilities and promises of God. After all, they think it's all up to God anyway, as if they are simply pawns in the game. They know God as Rescuer but not as Sustainer. They believe God can but doubt He will in their situation.

True sons and daughters of the King understand that God's unlimited grace provides them with unlimited possibility and their faith provides the key. God is always willing to empower, bless, save, deliver and heal, but we must turn the key of faith and unlock His promises for our lives.

## Vision Activates Faith

Remember, God uses vision to activate faith in our hearts and imaginations. When He reveals something to us, He gives us the authority to pursue it and offers us His full support. We can walk confidently because we know our steps are being ordered by the Lord. That's a game changer.

Sadly, many Christians believe that because God knows what they need, He will provide it according to His timing without their participation in the process. Such theology replaces faith with hope alone and denies the need for our active participation. It causes endless waiting and, *"hope deferred makes the heart sick".* Faith activates hope, putting action with desire. Hope gives faith a context and direction. Hope dreams and envisions while faith reaches, believes, walks and pursues what's been promised by God.

## *The antidote to double-mindedness is faith-filled vision.*

Once our heart and mind connect in faith to what God shows us, anything is possible. And as we cultivate that connection, our faith will grow stronger. Tempting alternatives that once seemed viable will pale in comparison to the glory revealed by the Holy Spirit. Clear, prophetic vision from God empowers our walk of faith.

### The Power of Faith

The Bible teaches in Hebrews 11:6 NLT that *"Without faith, it's impossible to please God."* It's impossible because anything outside of faith originates with and depends on our own ability. We can't please God without coming into active agreement with what He's showing us by Holy Spirit revelation. It's impossible. Otherwise, we're left trying to keep all the rules and "live a good Christian life" with no power.

Remember, in Hebrews 11:1 KJV, Paul teaches that, *"Faith is the substance of things hoped for, the evidence of things not seen."* Faith is directly connected to what we place our hope in. If our hope is in ourselves, our abilities or simply hoping for good luck, we won't walk in God's best for us. Faith works best when it's pointed toward the dreams, desires and vision the Holy Spirit reveals. When we see and agree with God's agenda and turn our hearts toward what's on God's heart, the seeds of inspiration He gave us will grow, along with our faith.

Paul recounts the faith of Abraham in Romans 4:20-22 NLT, where it says, *"Abraham never wavered in believing God's promise. In fact, his faith grew stronger, and in this he brought glory to God. He was fully convinced that God is able to do whatever He promises. And because of Abraham's faith, God counted him as righteous."* Just like Abraham, we can become fully convinced in our hearts that God's promises for us are absolutely true, regardless of what we see or feel in the natural. But that's an intentional process we must pursue.

It's easier to wait on the God who parts the sea than walk with the God who's promised you the land on the other side. People love instantaneous miracles and moments of breakthrough. We want hands up, waves towering and Pharaoh's army instantly destroyed. And so we cry out for the God of breakthrough to show up and to rescue us from our mess. But rarely are people willing to cultivate an atmosphere of ongoing breakthrough where His abiding presence matures them from glory to glory. Where God reveals Himself not just as Rescuer but as the one who walks with us in the cool of the day, moment by moment.

It seems easier to pray for a miraculous revival than to walk in the fullness of the Kingdom that's living inside us now. Like the disciples who longed for Jesus to show up in a moment of power, we long for the powerful display. We desire political power and to conquer areas of society. We want a shakeup. Yet Jesus invites us to walk with Him in the fullness of the Kingdom, day by day, knowing lasting transformation comes one encounter at a time.

## A Movement of Moments

Don't get me wrong. I long to see more miracles. I love the Glory of God's presence. But I want more than moments in church services. Times of awakening and revival are beautiful sovereign moves of God—like spontaneous springs in the desert—where God decides in a moment to spring up out of nowhere and pour out more of His unlimited manifest presence in greater measure on a people. But we also have to learn how to walk in the reality of the Kingdom every day while we expectantly wait for these outpouring moments.

Even as I write this book, there is an incredible move of the Spirit that has begun at Asbury University in Kentucky. A spontaneous revival erupted out of a chapel service that is sparking hunger, repentance and worship all over the country. Praise God! However, as I read stories and watch testimonies of people who are there, so many are reporting that this is the first time they've ever experienced anything like this in their life. Many, like one man who said he'd been a believer for over 25 years say they have been in church their whole life and never experienced the kind of freedom in worship and tangible sense of God's presence they are feeling now. It reminds me of Wesley's Aldersgate story I shared earlier. Faithful but unfulfilled. Saved, but not satisfied.

As New Testament believers, we have a wonderful opportunity to hold in tension the reality of fullness in Christ while simultaneously asking God to enlarge our capacity to experience more of His presence. We are in Christ and He is in us, yet He is continuing to fill us with more of Himself each day. Such a beautiful mystery. One can't replace the other, but when they work in tandem, we experience a greater reality in the Kingdom. Completely satisfied in Christ yet hungry for more.

It's like being married. I am already married to my wife. We can't be more married than we already are. I know my wife loves me and she knows I love her completely and unreservedly. That's an established fact and we live from that reality. But I also know that there are depths in our relationship that will continue to unfold and be explored throughout our marriage as I pursue her heart. The same is true in the Kingdom. We can't be more saved than we already are, yet we continually seek to mine the depths of His unending fullness, forever.

I believe God wants our churches filled with His weighty presence and His people filled with hunger as they worship and pursue Him wholeheartedly. I believe He wants an ongoing movement of moments and miracles in the marketplace through His sons and daughters. Moments where His overflowing goodness spills out and onto everyone around. Where the demonstration of His Kingdom becomes our normal experience, not a periodic surprise.

I have known God as a Rescuer and Reviver, but I also want to know Him as a Sustainer. I have seen Him in miraculous moments of deliverance. Now I also long to see a movement of God's people walking with Him in the cool of the day. A people living in the supernatural fullness of their identity, design and assignment. Releasing God's transforming Love and performing miracles with Him, not just waiting to be rescued.

## Choose Your Adventure

I've found God often shows up in the way I perceive Him. That means we have a choice. We can view God the way we always have, or through eyes of faith. That doesn't mean God isn't there for us in moments of crisis. It simply means we need to enlarge our vision of who God really is so we can experience Him in new and exciting ways.

You can cry out for God to rescue you like the Israelites did, or you can walk in an atmosphere of continual breakthrough like Jesus. Wait for God to move in your city, or walk in your assignment and host a move of God. The choice is up to you. Personal revival is most often needed when we let the fire go out on the altar of our hearts. You and I are the only ones who are responsible for tending that fire.

It's very tempting to wait for a significant moment or catalyst to happen. Sometimes that moment happens. And when it does, that's great. But to wait endlessly on a moment to occur can lead to years of frustration on one hand and a tendency toward hype on the other.

However, there are several principles we can cultivate that will create an environment in and around your life where the Kingdom of God can flourish unhindered. Where you become a carrier of God's power and presence, instead of continually waiting on it to appear. Let's dive into each of these and set a foundation for exponential growth in your life.

## Cultivating an Awareness of His Presence

If you've been around church culture very long, you know there's a habit of gathering and then asking God to come be among His people. The implication is that God is otherwise occupied, but now we need Him to turn His attention to our church service. It may be tradition and spiritually sincere, but it has little to do with Kingdom truth and how we are to live in God's presence.

God is omnipresent, omniscient and omnipotent. In other words, He exists everywhere and in everything at all times. He knows everything about everything and has all power to do anything, anywhere, at any time. There is no place in the universe He does not already exist or have the knowledge, wisdom, understanding and power to affect change. Psalm 139:7-10 NLT, reminds us *"I can never escape from your Spirit! I can never get away from your presence! If I go up to heaven, you are there; if I go down to the grave, you are there. If I ride the wings of the morning, if I dwell by the farthest oceans, even there your hand will guide me, and your strength will support me."*

Without an understanding of the omnipresence of God, it's easy to think God is busy, off in some heavenly realm dealing with something more important than what we're going through. But that's not our God. Remember, Psalm 37:23-25 NLT, says, "*The LORD directs the steps of the godly. He delights in every detail of their lives. Though they stumble, they will never fall, for the LORD holds them by the hand. Once I was young, and now I am old. Yet I have never seen the godly abandoned or their children begging for bread.*"

He is everywhere and in every detail of our lives—right now. Closer than the air we breathe. More real than the chair we're sitting in. God is waiting for us to acknowledge He's here with us, in us and through us right now. He's been here all along. He never left and He has no plans to leave now. As we invite the Holy Spirit to awaken our hearts to that reality, He will fill us to overflowing. That's our God!

Central to cultivating an atmosphere of breakthrough is the reorienting of our hearts and minds to the fact that God is with us. Not just some of the time but all the time. And once we believe and live in this reality, we can tune the ears and eyes of our hearts to His Spirit. We can whisper a prayer in any moment. Lift up spontaneous praise for the most insignificant occurrence. Open our heart to His loving presence and worship Him anywhere at any time.

As you walk through your day, look for signs that He's at work. Listen for clues in your spirit that He is speaking, leading and directing you. Choose to see people and situations through the lens of His Kingdom. There is not one thing you are walking through that He has not allowed. Not one moment where He is not already present. Not one difficulty through which He has not already walked and prepared a way of deliverance and victory for you. That understanding is the foundation for living victoriously in the Kingdom.

To continue this process of awakening your heart to His presence, I suggest you start your days with gratitude. Thank Him that He already knows the end from the beginning. Thank Him that He alone is in control of all things. Thank Him that His Holy Spirit will faithfully lead you through every situation you will face. Thank Him for the divine appointments, supernatural encounters, suddenlies and special opportunities He is bringing you today. Declare your trust in Him and commit to follow wherever He leads. As you do, your heart will align with the presence of God who lives in and surrounds you.

## Renewing Your Mind

I've already talked a lot about renewing our minds, but I want to reinforce this concept once again as you make God's IDEAL your new normal. Remember, our view of God, His Kingdom and our place in it contextualizes what we see as possible. It creates a lens through which we interpret everything and a framework on which our lives are built. This is why cultivating an awareness of His presence, combined with renewing our mind is so powerful. Worship and gratitude focus our attention on Jesus rather than our situation. When we see life through the lens of His Word, rather than through the wounded lens of our experience and false expectations plagued by fear, our heart connects by faith to what

God reveals as possible, rather than on what seems impossible on our own.

Remember, you can be absolutely saved, love Jesus and be on your way to heaven yet be trying to do life in the Kingdom-based on an old broken framework. For generations the church has focused on behavior management to reduce or get rid of sinful actions instead of dealing with the roots of our broken thinking. You can get people to stop doing unwanted actions for a little while with guilt, shame and pressure, but lasting change will never happen through those means.

> *Enduring transformation happens when we install a new Kingdom-based framework for living in our heart and mind.*

Every time the Holy Spirit reveals His truth in stark contrast to your history and present reality, repent. Change your mind. Come out of agreement with your old way of thinking and into agreement with God's Kingdom truth. Using the 5R's I taught you earlier, be intentional to take every thought captive. Compare what you're feeling, thinking and believing to the truth of God's Word. This will align your heart and mind with what God has already declared as true. Your actions and reactions will be transformed, not by pure will, trying harder or behavior management, but by the power of the Holy Spirit.

## Pray in Faith

One of the best ways to operate the levers of our renewed minds is to pray God's Word and stand on the completed work of the cross. For most people, this is a monumental shift because they've been taught to approach God as a beggar. They beg God to show up. Beg Him to rescue them. Beg for scraps from His table. Praying that way for decades constructs an inner framework of belief that has very little to do with the God of the Bible and how the Kingdom works.

I used to play with tinker toys for hours as a kid and loved all the complex structures I could create. As I've learned more about how God designed our minds to work, I now know that thoughts turn into beliefs which turn into actions. And, repeated actions turn into habits that produce fruit. In simple terms, our thoughts, beliefs and actions are like individual pieces of a tinker toy set. The more connections we make, the faster a structure is built. As that structure is formed over many years, it becomes the operating system for our life. That's why we must make sure we're building the right kind of structure inside our mind. Will it be one that aligns with the truth of God's Word or one that aligns with our experiences, opinions and the wounds of the past? If we are not intentional, we'll end up with a life we never intended.

But consider this. What if you prayed like every prayer was already answered? What if praying by the Spirit was designed to raise our awareness that God has already provided every need a heavenly solution? And praying was simply God's way of inviting us to see things from His perspective—a way to bring His perfectly designed solution into our situation? What if praying is about declaring and affirming God's ability and not our inability? That would change everything. It would construct a new framework within our minds based on how the Kingdom works.

Think about what we commonly call, "The Lord's Prayer" in Matthew 6:9-13 NKJV where Jesus says; *"In this manner, therefore, pray: Our Father in heaven, hallowed be Your name. Your Kingdom come. Your will be done on earth as it is in heaven. Give us this day our daily bread. And forgive us our debts, as we forgive our debtors. And do not lead us into temptation but deliver us from the evil one. For Yours is the kingdom and the power and the glory forever. Amen."*

Everything Jesus says to pray for in this prayer has already been accomplished on our behalf in the New Covenant. Think about it. We don't cry out to God as a deserted orphan. No! We pray to the Father as His restored child, not as a beggar without hope. His Kingdom has come and continues to come through the work of Jesus. His will is being accomplished right now through sons and daughters who see and agree with Him. He's already provided us an abundance of unlimited "bread" we need to live and thrive. We're not just horrible old sinners hoping to get into heaven one day. No! Through Jesus and His work on the cross, we have been forgiven by the Father so we can freely forgive others. Instead of barely hanging on, hoping God will rescue us from the attacks of the enemy, we're thanking God for His provision and deliverance from the attacks of the enemy. In Christ, we have overcome. It's settled.

He is down every road, around every corner, over every hill waiting for us with everything we need for our journey. He has made a way, cleared every path and provided every tool, resource, idea and opportunity to accomplish all He created us for. Therefore, when you pray, you must believe that what you are asking for is already accomplished in Christ. It's already yours. You're not praying like a beggar; but as God's child who has already received what you asked for. As Jesus said in Mark 11:24 NLT, "*I tell you, you can pray for anything, and if you believe that you've received it, it will be yours.*"

## Create Space

To create space for the vision God has placed in our hearts we need to let go of our old, preconceived ideas about what life can look like in exchange for all God has promised. Even though it is often painful. Otherwise, we will have no room to receive what's coming.

Anytime God asks us to lay something down or give something up, it's because He has something better for us.

*The most fruitful things from our last season are often the biggest barriers to our fruitfulness in the next.*

That often doesn't make sense to us, so we end up holding on to good things whose season has expired.

*Trusting God always requires an exchange.* A "not my will but yours be done" moment of reckoning. Even though the exchange is a painful stretch and our flesh pushes back, we know it's always worth it. God always leads us into greater depths of joy, peace, presence and glory. He offers us more than we can ask or think if we'll just trust Him and give Him our yes, "lay down our nets" and follow Him. Just like the early disciples, following Jesus requires a choice. Their nets were deeply connected to their identity—who they were and what they did—defining their place in society and among each other. Their nets brought joy, freedom and offered the promise of provision. All good things. Yet Jesus commanded them to lay them down in exchange for something that didn't initially make sense. You have a choice to lay down your nets or keep fishing.

## Invest in Your Assignment

The gifts of God are like precious diamonds. But they don't often look like that at first. Diamonds don't emerge from the dirt cut, set and polished. There is a transformation process that have to go through that brings out their brilliance and potential. It's the same with us. It takes intentional, Spirit-led work and we need to be willing to ask ourselves the hard questions.

Do you have the skills you need to get to where you believe God is calling you? Do need a mentor? Could you use some training in a specific area and are you willing to invest in your assignment as a key part of your Kingdom growth?

Many people have shared their dreams with me and their belief that God called them to pursue it but they're unwilling to invest the time, energy, focus and finances to make it happen. They want an instant

*The promises of God*
*most often come*
*to us as opportunities that*
*require our response.*

manifestation of their dream without the process of development required to walk in it. It takes preparation and personal investment to see God's IDEAL come into full maturity. The promises of God most often come to us as opportunities that require our response.

Investing in our journey is like a farmer who must sow seeds to get a harvest. If he doesn't sow the seeds, he won't reap a harvest, no matter how much he desires it. When we step forward in faith, boom! Breakthrough happens. Investing in our assignment can unlock the door of promise and bring us huge benefits and blessings. Like a boomerang, the blessing of God comes back around in ways we could never imagine. Blessed, multiplied and accelerated. When we do what it takes to learn, grow and build what God has called us to, it yields huge results.

Don't allow doubt, fear and lack to boomerang back into your life— one step forward, two steps back. I've mentored many emerging entrepreneurs who have experienced both dynamics in their life and business. The ones who choose to operate by faith see the results of God's Kingdom show up. They experience provision and divine appointments, creative ideas and innovative strategies. And the ones who choose to play small, allowing fear to thwart their movement toward a God-given dream, see mostly frustration. They feel as if they are always starting over, never able to catch a break. That's not God's ideal.

Investing in our calling also requires sacrifice. David said in 2nd Samuel NKJV, "*I will not offer the Lord that which cost me nothing*". Sometimes that's money and we need to sacrificially invest in learning something for the next stage in our journey—like an online course, a professional certificate or college degree. Other times we need to take a risk or do something new. Regardless,

*Growth happens when we're willing to place more faith in the promise of God than what we see in the natural.*

People that aren't willing to let go or try something new, end up stuck in the same place, holding onto a promise with potential opportunity, yet frustrated and depressed.

Investing in our calling also requires walking with the right people. 1 Corinthians 4:15, reminds us we will have a lot of teachers but not many fathers. In other words, a lot of people will offer their two cents on what you should be doing, but there aren't many people who will invest in your journey for the long term. Every person I know who is growing in their journey—whether in business, the arts or any other realm of society—intentionally invests in key relationships for the purpose of mutual growth. You can try to figure it all out on your own, or you can receive the relationship gifts God brings into your life to bless you and make you a blessing. Investing in your calling requires walking with the right people and not just doing the right thing.

Throughout my journey, God has brought specific people into my life for specific reasons. Could God have taught me those things supernaturally by His Spirit? Sure! But He chose to bring a person. Why? Because the Kingdom is all about relationships. It's about learning to walk with and receive from one another. Relationships are where life is exchanged and influence happens. We gain more than just knowledge and facts through our relationships. We gain the wisdom and understanding we need to use that knowledge effectively. And we are refined and sharpened in the process. Remember, God's Word says in Proverbs 27:17 NIV, *"As iron sharpens iron, so one person sharpens another."*

We need to be keenly aware of who God brings into our lives. Some are for us to learn from, some to learn with and some to teach. Many of the teachers and influencers God has brought in my life over the years gave me the knowledge I needed to step into the next thing God called me to. Many of them weren't believers but God used what they carried to equip me to for the next part of my journey.

God has blessed me with wonderful friends, key people to walk and grow with. I call them my running buddies. We regularly set apart time to encourage one another, share and learn. They are the people I trust, who I give access to and allow to speak correction, concern and encouragement into my life.

There are also those in my journey who I invest in by sharing what I've learned. Some are paid relationships like people who participate in our mentoring program, courses and conferences—while others are naturally occurring friendships. As we are faithful to pour out, God is faithful to pour in.

## Be Teachable

Being teachable is the heart posture that allows us to receive from others what God has for us. Thinking we know it all and don't need anyone's help is a sure way to end up frustrated and in turmoil. Why reinvent the wheel when God has already provided others with the solutions you need?

Hosea 4:6 NIV says, *"my people perish for lack of knowledge"*. Perishing is the natural result of not knowing what to do. And again, Proverbs 24:3,4 NKJV says, *"through wisdom a house is built, by understanding it's established and by knowledge the rooms are filled with pleasant and precious riches."*

We need wisdom and the understanding of how, when and where to execute. In business, it's not enough just to know the latest trend or marketing techniques. And, in life, it's not enough to live off the latest inspirational lifehack from social media. We need Spirit-birthed understanding combined with practical knowledge. Information alone does not equal transformation, it's information plus interaction with the Lord and others. That's when real change begins to happen.

## Develop Spiritual Grit

Spiritual grit is the result of a transformed mind. Ephesians 6:13 NKJV says, *"...and having done all, stand."* When the going gets tough and life is confusing, or you don't understand why this or that isn't working—call on the Lord, lean into His voice and stand. You will never make lasting progress in your life, much less your Kingdom assignment if you aren't willing to keep going when the going gets rough. The winds of confusion and doubt will surround you and knock you off course if you don't develop spiritual grit.

Of course, you're going to fail. Of course, you're going to have setbacks. Everything is not going to turn out the way you thought. That's normal. Just because something is a bit difficult, doesn't mean it's not God! Anytime we're walking in the fullness of what God has for us, there is going to be resistance. But Proverbs 24:16 NKJV says, "the righteous man may fall seven times, and rises again...." We aren't defined by the number of times we fail or fall. God is the one who defines us. Our willingness to get back up and keep going every time we experience a setback is what helps us develop spiritual grit.

**When you experience a big success, you can't get lazy and lean back on your own abilities. Same thing when you experience failure. Don't let your feelings rule in a moment of defeat. As David said in Psalm 42:5 NIV, you must encourage yourself in the Lord, saying, "Why so downcast, O my soul, why so disturbed within me? Put your hope in God, for yet will I praise Him, my Savior and my God." In the middle of it all, set your eyes on the goal, put your hope in God and keep going.**

## Seek Out Community

Years ago, I worked at a summer camp in Dahlonega, Georgia. I remember one night in particular. We were sitting around a campfire when one of the senior leaders pulled some coals out of the fire pit and set them aside. Later, the leader taught us a great life lesson. He shared how being with our friends at camp was like a piece of wood that was fueled by a fire. But when we go back home, we were going to have times when we would lose our fire's passion, like the coals he had separated from the fire. It was at those times we needed to seek out community.

A transparent, authentic community offers us the strength and support that going it alone cannot give us. But for many, being a part of a community is not their normal way of living. That's why it must be an intentional act that comes from a renewed mind. In fact, Paul encourages the church to renew their minds in Romans 12 immediately before He instructs them about walking with each other in the context of love and their role in the Body of Christ.

## *Renewing your mind enables you to walk in love with others while cultivating unity.*

When we intentionally renew our mind to God's truth, we see life from His perspective. We see others through His eyes. We embrace our place in the Body of Christ as vital to the well-being of the whole, not as the star of the show. We are enabled by His Spirit to be patient, kind, long-suffering and filled with grace.

In the Body of Christ, every joint is meant to supply what we each need but too often, during seasons of failure, people retreat into isolation instead of seeking out someone with whom they can be transparent and honest. Seeking help when times are hard is not a sign of weakness. It's a sign of humility and an invitation to bear one another's burdens, as Galatians 6 encourages.

Just like it says in Proverbs 27:17, *"iron sharpens iron"*. We need each other to spark, challenge and sharpen one another. Hebrews 10 says we are to, *"spur one another on to love and good works."* Going it alone is a recipe for disaster. We may make it for a little while, but eventually our fiery passion will fade. We need others to live in the fullness of God's Kingdom.

Community is also very important when you're learning to hear God's voice. A loving community of like-minded believers who can help us discern if what we're hearing is from God is vital. Otherwise, it's too easy to stay in our own bubble of belief. Sort of like living in a vacuum. The Bible says in Proverbs 27:9 that there's safety in an abundance of counselors. Others can help us hear God's voice and walk in a place of safety and protection.

## Resist Comparison

One of the most reliable strategies the enemy uses to derail our walk and assignment is comparison. Everyone else's life seems to be a perfectly curated social media profile. No mistakes. No weaknesses. No areas of immaturity. No tough learning experiences. No fear. Only success after success. Though we know what we see is not the whole story, the enemy uses their images of success against us, reminding us of it every time we experience difficulty. Suddenly, our life seems ordinary. Our journey seems slower and our wins are not as big. Every failure is magnified.

When the enemy tempts you to play the comparison game, I encourage you to do one thing. Be thankful. Start thanking the Lord for all He's done in your life and all He's brought you through. Thank Him for the victories and for the promises of things yet to come. Next, thank Him for the way He's moving in the lives of your friends. Especially the ones the enemy is comparing you to. Thank God for their faithfulness. Pray for their protection and encouragement. Declare the promises of God over their life and calling. As you do, the enemy will lose all ability to torment you and you win.

There will always be people who experience life at different speeds. For some, the breakthrough comes quickly in one area and slower in another. Neither is a reflection of God's Love or His desire to bless them. It's just a reflection of their journey.

## Keep Jesus at the Center

As we walk by faith, Jesus will often show us ways to do things that will increase our productivity, accelerate our progress and multiply our efforts. But it's important to remember Jesus said HE is THE Way and HE will reveal the truth to us about each situation we face, person we encounter. Each difficulty or success that comes our way will strengthen our discernment, reveal motives and bring clarity.

It's easy to attach our hearts to the ideas and opportunities, resources and relationships that God provides us with. They are tangible and seen. But when we do, we settle for less than what God intended. The blessings and benefits of the Kingdom are for our good. They enable us to accomplish our assignment, fulfill the desires of our heart and become conduits of blessing to others—but they do not define us. Nor do they replace our need for Jesus. The more blessing we walk in, the more vital it is we gather it all up and lay it at the feet of Jesus, our daily act of worship.

If at any point (and it can be subtle) our heart becomes more connected to what has been provided than to the Provider himself, adjustment is required. Otherwise, we'll find ourselves depending on the tools God gave us rather than the tool Giver. Gaining identity and strength from our accomplishments, rather than from our Heavenly Father.

*Be thankful for the provision*
*but put your trust in the Provider.*

The temptation is to trust in the latest methodology, resource, revelation, or what we see working and ride it until the wheels fall off. But Jesus calls us to Himself through daily connection. He encourages us to pray, "Give us this day, our daily bread" instead of relying on our past successes. As you offer your heart and life to Him, you release the pressure of performance and reconnect to God as your Source.

Trust the Lord for today and choose not to worry about tomorrow. Put everything into His hands and walk by faith, trusting Him to establish your steps as you walk together. Every idea, opportunity, resource and relationship is from God and for His glory. Ask Him to show you which tools you need and which ones to let go of. Your load will become lighter and your heart freed to fully pursue His plans for your life.

## Final Thoughts

As we end this journey together, realize this is just the beginning. You now know what Kingdom living can look like if you choose to walk in God's IDEAL. As you employ the principles we've covered, you'll experience an atmosphere of breakthrough in your life and begin to experience the favor and provision of God in ways you never have before. You'll become a carrier of breakthrough instead of waiting on it to happen. A divinely created intersection point where heaven meets earth and transformation occurs as you walk in God's IDEAL.

Cultivate your identity in Christ. Explore and uncover your unique design. Be faithful to all God has given you and trust Him for expansion at the right time. Watch expectantly for God's hand. He will align you with the right people and the right resources at the right time. Both for your assignment and your refinement. And finally, walk daily rooted and grounded in the Love of God. Choose to see your life from His perspective.

When you face challenges along your way, remember that God has promised in 2 Corinthians 12:9 NIV that *"His grace is sufficient for us, because His power is made perfect in our weakness." Don't hide your weakness and feelings of inadequacy from the Lord. Instead, bring them before Him as an offering. Make a divine exchange— your weakness for His strength.*

Lastly, remember you're in a battle and it's going to take some intentionality to win. Jesus has already won the war, but there are many battles we each must face each day as we step into God's promises. We are not called to live life in our own strength, but in the power of His might. As sons and daughters in the Kingdom, He has provided us all the strength and resources we need to walk victoriously with Him.

In Ephesians 6, Paul ends his letter to the church at Ephesus by encouraging them to put on the full armor of God. I encourage you to do the same:

*"A final word: Be strong in the Lord and in His mighty power. Put on all of God's armor so that you will be able to stand firm against all strategies of the devil. For we are not fighting against flesh-and-blood enemies, but against evil rulers and authorities of the unseen world, against mighty powers in this dark world, and against evil spirits in the heavenly places.*

*Therefore, put on every piece of God's armor so you will be able to resist the enemy in the time of evil. Then after the battle you will still be standing firm. Stand your ground, putting on the belt of truth and the body armor of God's righteousness. For shoes, put on the peace that comes from the Good News so that you will be fully prepared. In addition to all of these, hold up the shield of faith to stop the fiery arrows of the devil. Put on salvation as your helmet, and take the sword of the Spirit, which is the word of God.*

*"Pray in the Spirit at all times and on every occasion. Stay alert and be persistent in your prayers for all believers everywhere."* Ephesians 6:10-18 NLT

Revisit these principles daily and use them as a framework for living the IDEAL Kingdom life God designed for you. And when you hit a rough spot in your journey, remember you are not alone. You're God's child, He's for you and He's given you everything you need to thrive. You are more than a conqueror through Christ Jesus. You were created to overcome. You were created to thrive.

I love you, my friend. And I look forward to seeing you on the journey.

# About the Author

Matt Tommey is an author, artist, entrepreneur, and mentor who is passionate about helping people live in the abundance of God's Kingdom. Through his personal growth journey and extensive work mentoring artists, Matt learned how to make Kingdom principles easy to understand and apply to everyday life so anyone can experience abundant life in Christ.

He currently lives in East Texas with his wife, Tanya, and their son, Cameron, where he enjoys life with friends and family, gardening, and creating original artworks.

Since 2009, Matt has primarily mentored artists who want to thrive spiritually, artistically and in business. He is a successful entrepreneur, popular conference speaker, podcast host (The Thriving Christian Artist), author of 7 books for Kingdom creatives and is recognized internationally as a leader in creativity and the arts. Through his new book, God's Plan for Living, Matt is taking the Kingdom principles he's learned in mentoring artists and sharing them with the world.

# Your Next Steps

Thanks so much for reading this book! I pray it was a big blessing in your life.

If so, it would really bless me if you would take a moment to do three things:

1. Review the book on Amazon.

2. Share the book with your friends on social media.

3. Visit **www.GodsPlanForLiving.com** to request your free downloadable copy of God's Promises Daily Affirmation guide.

Doing all of these helps us spread the word about God's Plan for Living.

Thanks!

*Matt*

# Other Resources from Matt Tommey

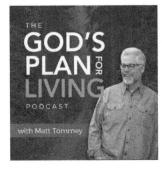

### The God's Plan for Living Podcast

Matt's weekly podcast, full of practical truth from God's Word, his own life and experience and from the book, God's Plan for Living can be found at Podcast.GodsPlanForLiving.com

### Other Books by Matt Tommey

To see Matt's full line of books, visit MattTommeyMentoring.com/Resources

### To Stay Connected to Matt and God's Plan for Living

Be sure to visit our website at

## www.GodsPlanForLiving.com

Made in the USA
Middletown, DE
03 May 2023